Each Other's Angels

Each Other's Angels

Practicing Personalism
as a Catholic Worker Tradition

Toni Flynn
Foreword by Jeff Dietrich

RESOURCE *Publications* • Eugene, Oregon

EACH OTHER'S ANGELS
Practicing Personalism as a Catholic Worker Tradition

Copyright © 2016 Toni Flynn. All rights reserved. Except for brief quotations in critical publications or reviews, no part of this book may be reproduced in any manner without prior written permission from the publisher. Write: Permissions, Wipf and Stock Publishers, 199 W. 8th Ave., Suite 3, Eugene, OR 97401.

Resource Publications
An Imprint of Wipf and Stock Publishers
199 W. 8th Ave., Suite 3
Eugene, OR 97401

www.wipfandstock.com

PAPERBACK ISBN: 978-1-4982-0533-7
HARDCOVER ISBN: 978-1-4982-8301-4
EBOOK ISBN: 978-1-4982-6887-5

Manufactured in the U.S.A.

For my Guardian Angels

Father Tom Weston, S. J.
Father Mike Cicinato
Sister Theresa Harpin, C. S. J.

and in memory of

Father Daniel Berrigan, S. J.

We are each other's angels—we meet when it is time.
We keep each other going—and we show each other signs.

—Chuck Brodsky

Contents

Foreword by Jeff Dietrich | ix
Author's Preface | xv
Acknowledgements | xxi

Part I—Overviews

Come Follow Me, a Catholic Worker Introduction | 3

Personalism, Emmanuel Mounier, and the Catholic Worker Movement | 6

St. Benedict and Dorothy Day | 8

A Few Words About the High Desert Catholic Worker | 10

The Salvation Army Homeless Project | 12

Roy Bourgeois and the SOA | 15

Overview of Toni's Arrest, Trial, and Jails in Georgia | 17

Glimpses of Life in a Southern Jail | 19

Part II—Essays

Chapter 1—The Mean Streets and the Desert | 31
    A Guy Named Joe | 32
    A Woman of No Importance | 34
    Alan: Food and Company | 37
    Angela | 40

Beggar Bowl Woman | 42
Bill: A Veteran With Nothing Left To Lean On | 45
Doc: Looking For Hope Beyond the Hype of the Season | 47
Exiles In the Desert, Part I | 50
Exiles In the Desert, Part II | 53
Fond Farewell to a Noble Friend | 55
Imagine William's World | 59
Michael: Soap Box Prophet | 63
People With Habits | 65
Tiffany: Mary's Word Resounding From the Maryland Hotel | 69
Walter: A Baptism of Beans | 73

Chapter 2—Protests and Jails | 76
Alice: Angel Under the Broom Tree | 76
Dora Jean Raises the Cross in Jail | 80
Jerry, Phil and Dan | 82
Kaya and Tammy: Lessons in Lockdown | 86
Kimberly in Ordinary Time | 89
Miss Wanda | 92
Officer C. | 95
Opal Takes On the System | 100
Pentagon Man | 101
Shannon, Eric, Toni and Elvis, Part I | 105
Shannon, Eric, Toni and Elvis, Part II | 107
Shannon Faces Chemo and Joanne Meets the Judge | 109
Sister Louise | 116
Stranger In the Night | 120
The MPO | 123
The Screaming Man | 126
Waiting In the Belly of the Beast for My Grandson's Birth | 128

Afterword by Eduard Loring | 133
We Are Each Other's Angels by Chuck Brodsky | 136

Foreword

'Bleeding Hearts' is most often a term of derogation hurled by some political conservatives at their liberal opponents. While Toni Flynn's radical (meaning deeply rooted) non-violent spirituality does not fit the narrow confines of liberal politics, her view of the world is in truth that of a 'bleeding heart'. Toni is a 'bleeding heart' because as a spiritual seeker, she writes from her own woundedness, about the woundedness of others, the broken systems, the hard heartedness of most of its acolytes, and the unexpected, serendipitous wonder of discovering a "pearl of great price" amidst the detritus of human existence.

Toni's vision of justice and compassion is formed by the Scriptures and inspired by the Catholic Worker Movement of Dorothy Day and Peter Maurin. Through her stories, she indicates to us how in her often seemingly insignificant, ineffectual efforts to be an angel to others, she does not seek success but rather, as Mother Teresa often remarked, she seeks faithfulness. "Catholic Workers do not aspire to be successful." she writes, "It is all about faithfulness. Perhaps we are fools trying to do what the rich man in the Gospel story could not do when Jesus invited him to leave all that was familiar, get rid of unnecessary possessions, give to the poor and follow..."

Following Jesus, going to the places of cultural darkness and brokenness, Toni inevitably takes us through troubling and troublesome terrain—the desert, homeless encampments, jails and prisons and seedy hotels like the Maryland in the roughest area of

Foreword

downtown San Pedro where "Cockroaches and mice were a nuisance but the rent was cheap and it beat sleeping on the sidewalks."

In the misery of that hotel, Toni meets Tiffany who had dropped out of college to care for her incarcerated sister's three young children, seeing that they had a roof over their head, clothes to wear, schooling, enough to eat and a place to sleep even if that meant standing in the San Pedro Catholic Worker food line for their evening meal and sleeping on the floor at night so that the boys could sleep on the only bed.

In Tiffany's self-sacrificing devotion to her nephews, Toni perceived a holy vision of Mary. "I tried to explain to Tiffany that because of her 'yes' to love, nurture, and provide for her sister's children, she was a true descendent of Mary. I did my best to assure her that an angel of God rustled protective wings over her each night as she lay down on the floor of her room and whispered into her ear while she slept: "You are full of grace and the Lord is with you." "

Toni's continued journey of compassion and justice takes us to the dreary, dangerous jail cells of Georgia where, as a prisoner of conscience, she avoids despair because of caring preacher women, supportive visitors, inspiring letters from all over the world, and the miracle of being housed next door to her friend and SOA co-conspirator, Franciscan priest, Jerry Zawada. Though separated by a thick concrete wall, Jerry and Toni were able to communicate with each other through a vent located near the ceiling that could only be accessed by standing on their respective toilets. Thus their conversations came to be called "toilet talks"!

When Jerry heard an announcement on a public radio station over his transistor radio that their prophetic friend and resistance hero, Philip Berrigan, had died of cancer, Toni writes "Jerry and I begin to pray the Rosary for the repose of Phil Berrigan's soul and for the members of his surviving family. We murmur back and forth to each other the Our Fathers and Hail Marys of the Glorious Mysteries and we can almost hear Phil's voice resonating with our own..."

Not only did Toni serve time in jail but also, in a most unlikely scenario, was sometime later hired by San Luis Obispo County

Foreword

Jail's Psychiatric Services under the direction of the Sheriff, to work primarily with incarcerated women. She writes how she was initially shocked to be given the position thinking that her own arrest record and incarceration would be a detriment. However, the hiring board that included a female custody lieutenant seemed to think that Toni's history was an asset for understanding the needs of inmates. One does not expect such insight from the leadership of regulation bound custody personnel but Toni's personality and honesty prompted them to hire her.

Toni writes about one particular inmate she worked with at the jail, who wanted, not medication or release assistance, but just to talk and be heard. "I learned that the best way to lighten her burden was to let her 'be'—be sad, be scared, be remorseful, be resentful, be resigned, be strong, be hopeful, be at peace. And then she stopped coming . . . " Toni took it a little personally when she first learned that the woman decided to join a Bible study group during the time slot previously set aside for meetings with Toni. However Toni worked it through and before her release, the woman returned, offering her a "Jesus People" flyer from the Bible class. When Toni read the flyer, she was struck by the sentence, "We simply argue that the Cross be raised again in the jailhouse and at the center of the market place as well as on the steeple of the church." realizing that the young woman was encouraging her to continue ministering to others in the jail.

It is significant that although Toni's visible persona is genuinely vivacious and convivial, just below the surface lie remembrances of pain and vulnerability that are the foundation of her 'bleeding heart' life choices. As a child, she was raised on the edge of poverty in a home riddled with paradox, where acute alcoholism and outbursts of aggression unfolded side by side with expressions of love, boisterous moments of humor and the gift of a Catholic education.

As an adult, Toni survived a divorce and completed the Catholic annulment process, later remarking to me that it served as a deep and necessary examination of conscience. She thereafter struggled financially as a single mother of four children, fending off periodic bouts of depression and choosing to work in situations

Foreword

where she could simultaneously support a family and serve others. A decade ago, she fell deeply in love and experienced the hope and heartbreak of a brief second marriage. It is to her credit that she fondly recalls that episode of her life as "worth the risk" even though "till death do us part" and "happily ever after" eluded her.

While working on this book, Toni began feeling doubts about herself as a writer. She sent me a letter saying, "Even though the stories I've written are my honest reflections about people who have touched my life, in some ways I feel like a fraud. People may read the book and conclude that I'm on a path to holiness when I know that I'm more adept at contradiction than I am at being holy."

Toni goes on to say, "It's true that I'm sadly aware of the shadow dimensions of my church and disturbed by my country's obvious hypocrisies, becoming more and more outraged by U.S. military decisions and actions. Yet, I remain a practicing Catholic and still retain my U.S. citizenship. I am not an agnostic nor am I an anarchist. I attend Mass. I vote. I get a lump in my throat whenever I hear someone sing Ave Maria or This Land Is Your Land."

During any period of her life, Toni Flynn could have resorted to a superficial lifestyle, or succumbed to cynicism and despair. But she repeatedly gives herself over to a deeper power of the Spirit that has imparted to her the creative wisdom and ability to raise four children, welcome seven grandchildren, accept personal losses, seek out the lost and lonely among us, do time as a prisoner of conscience, and write this brilliant book. As you will see, she fearlessly exposes her flaws while forging a conduit of compassion that connects her to the wounded human condition and allows her to hope for a better world.

This is indeed a book that will invite the stony hearted to crack open and inspire 'bleeding hearts' everywhere to carry on because, like all exceptional books of great depth, this one is written in blood . . .

Jeff Dietrich

Jeff Dietrich is editor of the Catholic Agitator *newspaper and the author of three books,* Reluctant Resister, Broken And Shared, *and* the Good Samaritan. *For over 45 years, Jeff and his wife Catherine Morris have been dedicated members of the Los Angeles Catholic Worker Community. http://lacatholicworker.org*

Author's Preface

A year after the end of World War II, I was counted amongst the first of the Baby Boomers, born into a family tribe of turbulent Irish-Italian Catholics in Santa Monica, California. I was a curious child, an idealistic teen, never finished college, never sustained a loving, life long marriage (although I tried twice!), never managed to learn a second language or how to swim the length of a pool, never earned a lot of money, and lived most of my life in rented houses.

Beginning in early childhood, I seemed destined to seek out and serve people in need of some sort of heart-felt compassion. A family story goes that when I was five years old, I invited a traveling salesman—a perfect stranger—inside our house while my mom was hanging laundry in the back yard. Apparently, I later told my mother that he looked thirsty so I asked him, would he like to have some of my chocolate milk or a bottle of my dad's beer? At gatherings for years thereafter, my parents told and retold the punch line—he passed on the milk, drank two bottles of beer and left without delivering his sales pitch.

I cherished every minute of my Catholic education from kindergarten through twelfth-grade. The nuns who taught me held me in high regard and I them. I was very devout, regularly examining my conscience and confessing my sins, receiving Holy Communion at Sunday Mass, reciting the Mysteries of the Rosary and singing hymns in the Latin choir. I hopelessly daydreamed about chivalry and romance; cried when I read Jane Eyre and

Author's Preface

Great Expectations; swooned over T.V. reruns of Gene Kelly dancing with a light post in Singing in the Rain. Most of all, I loved writing poems and stories and I even won a few writing contests in high school.

When I was twenty years old, naive and relatively clueless about matters of the heart, I married my high school crush. A year later, he became a policeman and I became a mother. I had four children by my thirtieth birthday. At thirty-one, I was a divorced working mom struggling to raise two sons and two daughters while also attempting to (yee-gads!) emotionally mature. Fortunately, my children, having survived my imperfect parenting, still like to hang out with me and have themselves become amazing adults, spouses and parents, contributing to the betterment of the world, each in their own way.

As a thirty-something year old single parent, not yet fully recovered from the impact of divorce, my pastor arranged care for my kids and sent me with a group of parishioners to volunteer for a morning at the Los Angeles Catholic Worker Hospitality Kitchen on Skid Row. I suppose it's safe to say that I finally began to really grow up that day, handing out slices of buttered bread to hundreds of homeless men and women. I knew by the last loaf of bread that I would return to Skid Row and that I would answer a call to practice the Works of Mercy and find a place in the Catholic peace and justice movement.

I owe the unfolding of my writing vocation to two men I met while chopping onions at the Hospitality Kitchen—Jeff Dietrich and Ray Correio. Thanks to their encouragement, I began publishing essays in the Catholic Agitator and Jeff still accepts my essays for publication. In 1989, Sand River Press published my first book (Finding My Way, A Journey Along the Rim of the Catholic Worker Movement), a compilation of essays originally printed in the Agitator between 1982 and 1988.

Toward the end of my fiftieth decade of life, I fell in love with a dear and long time friend. We shared a beautiful wedding in Ireland, a brief marriage, and a sad divorce. There is no denying that I felt a great sense of loss when that union ended yet the blessings

Author's Preface

I received remain intact like little twigs and bits of colored string woven together in a nest of memories. I believe that those blessings continue to flavor all aspects of my life, including my writing endeavors.

In 2014, after retiring from six years with San Luis Obispo County Jail Psychiatric Services, I made a pilgrimage to Assisi, Italy. There I knelt in the Church of San Damiano and asked God and St. Francis, "What next?" Weeks after my return home, I was hospitalized and underwent back surgery. Soon after my recovery, I was diagnosed with a severe episode of fatigue. My family doctor, a Catholic, suggested that maybe God's answer to "What next" was for me to slow down and rest. So I suspended my social and activist commitments, hibernating in my little rented bungalow much like a reclusive hermit. And in that stillness—that sacred pause—I began working on these stories.

Most of the essays in this book take up where my previous book left off, from way back in 1988 through the beginning of 2015. The people in each story and their circumstances are as I remember them, experientially and from notes. I am not an investigative journalist, nor am I a proficient historian; rather I paint with words, sincere and heartfelt portraits of transformative moments when other lives are interwoven with mine.

A few stories were previously published in modified versions in the Catholic Agitator. Many, however, remained for years in their original primitive note form, my thoughts and perceptions of unfolding events and encounters, hastily scribbled in pencil or ink onto tablets, paper bags, restaurant napkins, and the backs of used envelopes then messily filed away for years in a desk drawer. The exceptions being the facts I gathered from old newspaper clippings and the Internet about the construction and completion of Our Lady of the Angels Cathedral in downtown Los Angeles and the dismantling of the Veterans Wall at Mitchell Park in San Luis Obispo.

When I first pulled my dusty, unfinished stories out of the drawer and began to rewrite, revise, hone and polish them into a manuscript, I felt I had been reunited with old friends who had

Author's Preface

been waiting for me to walk through the portal leading to my soul so that I could fully embrace them.

The majority of stories focus on the years I worked with homeless people at The Salvation Army Homeless Project in San Luis Obispo and later, the years I lived as a volunteer at the High Desert Catholic Worker near Valyermo, where I encountered the desert poor, participated in protests against the School of the Americas and eventually served six months in jail in Georgia as a prisoner of conscience. However, some stories unfold during times I stayed with Catholic Workers on Skid Row, in San Pedro and Orange County. I also include tributes in honor of two friends who defy category—both of whom spent portions of time on duty as my personal 'earth angels'.

The essays are more or less arranged alphabetically by title rather than by date of authorship. With a few exceptions (those being people who gave me approval to use their full names or who have died), I use only first names in the essays. Some are actual first names and others were changed when I felt there was need for further anonymity.

In the Georgia correctional facilities I was confined to, most of the incarcerated women were African American and poor. There were a few white prisoners and it is of note that they were also poor. It's a poignant question as to whether it was an astonishing case of middle class and affluent white people never committing jail-worthy offenses or whether they were arrested less often because they had more money and influence, better legal representation and were treated with more forbearance by the courts.

Whatever the indications may be that some in Georgia's criminal justice system receive better legal treatment than others, there was no leniency for me as an out of state peace activist who had done an act of non-violent civil disobedience at a military base. The Federal criminal justice system in Georgia sentenced me to serve six months for a misdemeanor and thereafter I found myself, a white female (from California no less!), introduced into a predominantly African American southern jail culture. For the first time in my life, I was a member of a racial minority group

Author's Preface

and experienced what it feels like to be set apart in that way. Additionally, I was over fifty and the average age of female inmates was twenty-five. This further set me apart. Most of the women called me 'Miss Toni' and this, I learned in time, was in respectful deference to my age!

It's a delicate matter for a writer to distinguish groups or individuals by geographic regions, accents, race, religion, gender and age. Written language remains on the page and part of a writer's challenge is to foster respect for diversity rather than create further bias. With that said, in several stories, I refer to my African American cellmates and some of the church volunteers as Black. This is because I came right out and asked them how they racially and culturally identify themselves on documents and in conversation and they told me they prefer 'Black' (with a capital 'B' indicating a proper not generic term) rather than 'African American'. Also, when I quote them, I use their regional phraseology. One of my 'cellies' tried to teach me how to speak using colloquial expressions and after my sorry attempts she said to me, "You still so white!"

As you will read, I've kept company with men and women in dungeons and gutters, on the bitter streets and on the road to despair. Through my experiences accompanying homeless people and those locked away in our prisons and jails, I've come to discover serious flaws within our culture and within the corporate and governing systems of this country. I know that *liberty and justice for all* is not really *for all* because too many of the poor and marginalized among us remain illiterate, undernourished, medically and spiritually neglected, educationally disadvantaged, and often excluded, mistreated and misjudged.

I criticize, not because I don't value the positive aspects of the land of my birth, but in the hope that we as a nation will one day break through denial, sober up from our addictions to militarism and consumerism, examine our collective conscience, atone for past wrongs, urge our government officials to cease making policy decisions that perpetuate war, violence and the destruction of the environment. My Irish great grandparents and Italian grandparents were immigrants who arrived on U.S. soil from Ireland and

Author's Preface

Italy, dreaming of a better way of life and I certainly don't want to reject the citizenship they earned for me. However, as Albert Camus once stated, "I should like to love my country and still love justice."

Deep down inside of me, there remains a Pollyanna, polishing prisms so that they better refract light and throw rainbows into dark corners. And really, it's hope that keeps me going, not cynicism. I believe in Christ's Gospel message of love and forgiveness. I trust in the example of Dorothy Day and Peter Maurin who chose to practice personalism over communism, capitalism, and other "isms" that are grand in scope but all too often lacking in intimacy, integrity and connectedness.

I have taken that practice seriously by listening to amazing real life tales told to me by friends, acquaintances in the peace movement and comrades with questionable backgrounds who are denied a legitimate place in society—odd, obscure, peculiar, paltry, misbegotten, and out and out quirky folks who have left imprints on my heart. I offer these stories in the hope of inspiring readers to pray for and engage with people who most would consider to be 'undesirables'.

Not so deep down, I carry a proverbial trunk full of glaring contradictions, having spent as many hours watching British murder mysteries on T.V. as I have reading the Bible; having at times, envied people who own homes and enjoy financial security rather than feel confident in giving what I have to the poor and following in Jesus' footsteps; having in weak moments, allowed my temper to flare in the face of loved ones, forgetting my own promise to be a peaceful person. Nonetheless, I have tried my best to be an angel to others and have often accepted help from angels as well.

Acknowledgements

Writing a book is an incredibly lonely endeavor. For months, I hibernated in my bungalow, finishing this book as a tribute—begun years ago—to many of the unforgettable people who have blessed my life for the better. Yet I was never really alone, accompanied in spiritual and practical ways by so many I will never be able to properly thank them all.

The list includes Jeff Dietrich, my favorite writer and my good friend, a dedicated Los Angeles Catholic Worker, publisher of the Catholic Agitator and author of three books, who convinced me that this book was possible. Chris O'Connell, my friend for ages and an accomplished musician, who evolved as my editor, spending long hours reading and critiquing my first, second and third drafts until each story was ready to be born. In fact, I now affectionately refer to him as the midwife of my book!

Kudos are extended to Marjorie Collins, a fine graphic artist, who skillfully prepared the final manuscript and designed the front and back covers. I am so thankful to my dear friend, artist Julie Matey Conway, for the fine illustrations that grace this book, and to Chuck Brodsky for permission to include the lyrics to his song, *We Are Each Other's Angels*. Special acknowledgment to Deborah Kloiber, Head Archivist at St. Catherine University in St. Paul, Minnesota for permission to use Ade Bethune's art on the front cover. I am further grateful to two women writers, Heather King and Paula Huston, both of whom took a turn guiding me through the agonies and ecstasies of the writing process.

Acknowledgements

While serving six months as a prisoner of conscience, I would not have had the strength or focus to write stories of my experiences would it not have been for the loving support of John McAndrew, Jan Urban, Elizabeth Seward, Alice Budge, Ed Loring, Murphy Davis, Jerry Zawada, the L.A. Catholic Worker Community, Roy Bourgeois and the SOAWatch staff, and all those who wrote me letters. Special thanks to my son, David, who mailed L.A. Lakers' Basketball scores to me at the jail and to my son, Mark, who created a blog devoted to keeping others informed about the SOA and my incarceration.

I am indebted to the publishers and staff at WIPF and STOCK for believing my manuscript worthy of publication and for always being available to me throughout the course of publishing this book. I express my heartfelt gratitude to all the poets, prophets and pilgrims who have inspired my life and my writing, especially Daniel Berrigan. My prayer life is deepened and my creative spirit is lifted because of the monks at St. Andrew's Abbey in Valyermo, California. and the monks at the Monastery of the Risen Christ in San Luis Obispo, California. What centers me most is my family—my two siblings and their marriage partners, my four fabulous children and their spouses and—joy of joys—my seven awesome grandchildren. I am blessed with many angels!

PART I

Overviews

Come Follow Me

A Catholic Worker Introduction

For those of you who are wondering, the Catholic Worker is not an enterprise, not an organization, not a program, not a project. Like the sea, the wind, a Tango dancer, wild geese in flight, it is—in essence—a movement.

The aim of the Catholic Worker is to live in accordance with the justice and love of Christ. The sources of inspiration are the Hebrew and Greek Scriptures as handed down from the Catholic Church, and stories—recorded and retold—about the lives of the saints.

The Catholic Worker Movement began simply enough on May 1, 1933, in New York City, when a young Catholic convert (formerly a Bohemian journalist influenced by communistic ideals) named Dorothy Day teamed up with a French philosopher (a brilliant man in constant need of a bath!) named Peter Maurin to publish a newspaper called—you guessed it—The Catholic Worker.

The newspaper raised issues (and still does to this day) related to the scriptural promises of justice and mercy, the call to love the least of these (meaning Christ in the guise of the poor and marginalized), and the necessity of journalistic integrity in opposing the greed, oppression, and violence that haunts societies at home and abroad.

Before long, Dorothy was attracting volunteers and opening up a 'House of Hospitality' in New York City where the poor could come in from the streets, share meals, and feel welcome. She further dedicated herself to prayer, daily Mass, Benedictine spirituality and to an occasional arrest and jail term for non-violently resisting war and social injustice, the effects of which she saw as the exact opposite of love.

None of this was easy. "There are always answers", Dorothy said, "they are just not calculated to soothe." She was fond of quoting Dostoyevsky's Father Zossima: "Love in action is a harsh and dreadful thing compared to love in dreams."

Meanwhile, Peter broadened the tasks of assistance and resistance to include a better way of living via poetic vignettes and round table discussions promoting a return to small farming communities and village life. "The future of the Church—of God's people—is on the land." He believed that the cause of excessive consumerist acquisition for some at the expense of poverty and despair for others lay in society's alienation from the land.

Faithful consciences within the Catholic institutional structure, Dorothy and Peter were paradoxically radical and revolutionary challengers of the status quo of both Church and State—radical (from the Latin word 'Radix' meaning 'root') because they dug down to the roots of Christ's gospel message. They heard the Sermon on the Mount, they took it seriously, and they practiced it.

Theirs was a revolution of love, restoring human dignity to the least of our brothers and sisters. Theirs was a revolution of justice, exposing the societal systems that forfeited the spiritual virtues of compassion and mercy. Theirs was a green revolution fostering a respect for the earth itself, a renewed sense of the connectedness between people and the land.

Today, there are over 200 Catholic Worker Communities in the Americas, Europe, New Zealand, Australia and Africa. They are as diverse as the pilgrims who begin them, as committed to the experiments of voluntary poverty, non-violent resistance, community, the Works of Mercy, personalism (a Catholic Worker term preferred over capitalism and communism), manual labor, respect for the land, and prayer.

Catholic Workers do not aspire to be successful. There is not much concern over failure. It is all about being a moving presence. It is all about faithfulness. Perhaps Catholic Workers are fools. If so, it is about the foolishness of trying to do what the rich man in the gospel story could not do when Jesus invited him to leave all that is familiar, get rid of unnecessary possessions, give to the poor, and follow . . .

Personalism, Emmanuel Mounier, and the Catholic Worker Movement

Excerpts from a publication of Casa Juan Diego, Houston Catholic Worker, by Mark and Louise Zwick, August 1, 1999

Emmanuel Mounier, (French philosopher, 1905–1950) articulated the ideas of personalism, of human persons whose responsibility it is to take an active role in history, even while the ultimate goal is beyond the temporal and beyond human history. Mounier articulated it as a "philosophy of engagement... inseparable from a philosophy or transcendence of the human model." (Mournier, *Be Not Afraid*, Harper and Brothers).

People have found in the personalism of the Catholic Worker Movement a new vision and a way of life, a way to simply live the Gospels and their Catholic faith, and a model for a communitarian and personalist non-violent revolution to change the social order. Sometimes discouraged about the possibility of making any changes in our world, many have found in Peter Maurin and Dorothy Day people who are examples, witnesses to a vital, lively faith and holiness which translates into hospitality for the poorest of the poor and all the works of mercy, into work for peace, not waiting for the government or other agency structures to ponderously begin to do something, but who simply try to act as Jesus did, or as He asks His followers to do in the Sermon on the Mount and Matthew 25:31.

Peter Maurin introduced personalism and the ideas of Emmanuel Mournier to Dorothy Day and to the Catholic Worker Movement... however, when he introduced Mounier to the Worker, he did not present him as the very beginning of personalism in the Catholic Church. As Dorothy Day later mentioned, "Peter is always getting back to Saint Francis of Assisi, who was truly the 'great personalist.'" Peter knew that Mounier was bringing together the best of personalist ideas from the history and theology of the Church for this century.

To Mounier we owe the Catholic Worker emphasis on personal responsibility in history (not withdrawal from the world) applied by Maurin and Dorothy Day to the daily practice of the works of mercy... Mounier emphasized engagement in the world for the Christian, action, not isolation ... For personalists it is unthinkable that life, freedom and economics could be separated from responsibility, ethics and spiritual values. Love, rather than individualism, is the key.

St. Benedict and Dorothy Day

St. Benedict of Nursia was a Sixth century Italian monk who, after living by himself in a cave, founded and formed a monastic community, wrote and implemented a Rule for living wholesomely and prayerfully, day in and day out, within the structure of a monastery. The Rule of St. Benedict establishes a way of life rooted in the Gospel and grounded in scriptural principles of charity, humility, stability and faithfulness. Benedict had an uncanny understanding of human nature – its strengths as well as its weaknesses – and he knew well the need for balance in everyday life.

Benedictine monasteries have preserved and forwarded civilization over the centuries. They thrive to this day throughout the world and their spirituality has relevance to contemporary culture as well as speaking personally to individuals who long for an alternative to a materialistic way of thinking and being. Monastic life invites men and women to learn the value of work, prayer, study, community and the unique quality of hospitality that welcomes each guest as Christ. Some 1500 years after Benedict, there are still men and women who have completed formation and taken permanent vows to live in monasteries as brothers, priests and nuns.

Oblates are men and women dedicated to living out similar monastic values, remaining in their own residences as lay, clerical, single or married Christians who, after a period of formation, profess the "Act of Oblation" which establishes a formal association between them and a particular monastic community. Dorothy Day, some time after converting to Catholicism, embracing pacifism and co-founding The Catholic Worker Movement, became a Benedictine Oblate at St. Procopius Abbey in Lisle, Illinois in 1955. She was fifty-eight years old. It is easy to realize that long before she became an oblate, Dorothy was already reflecting, in her work with the poor and by her own prayer life, a kinship with Benedictine values and practices.

As for this author, it was no accident that I founded The High Desert Catholic Worker near St. Andrew's Benedictine Abbey in Valyermo, California. I instinctively knew that I would not be able to sustain a Catholic Worker lifestyle without integrating monastic practices into my daily life. Like Dorothy, I too took an Act of Oblation well past my fiftieth year of life and still adhere to Benedictine practices and values, returning when I can to St. Andrew's Abbey and frequenting The Monastery of the Living Christ in San Luis Obispo California, near my current home.

A Few Words About the High Desert Catholic Worker

The High Desert Catholic Worker began as a notion in my imagination. In 1999, I took a leap of faith. I quit my job at a retreat center on the California Central Coast and, with startup money from the Los Angeles Catholic Worker and generous friends, rented a desert house in Pearblossom about a seven-minute car drive from St. Andrew's Benedictine Abbey in Valyermo. At 3000 feet above sea level, the area is breathtakingly beautiful, blessed with Joshua trees, aromatic sage, phenomenal rock formations, wide vistas and clear skies. The region is also unmercifully hot in summer, with rattlesnakes, scorpions, fire ants and mountain lions inhabiting the terrain.

Manna House, as it was named, evolved into a modest retreat house. One or two at a time, weary inner city Catholic Workers from L.A. and Orange County, would arrive to enjoy the solitude and vastness of the high desert, attend Mass at the Abbey and have a room of their own wherein to sleep, read, rest and renew themselves for a few days.

Ministries began simply with the help of a few volunteers from nearby towns. Twice a week, we served coffee, bottled water, tortillas and oranges to Spanish speaking day laborers who gathered near the Pearblossom Highway, waiting for offers of farm or construction work. We also gleaned fruit from neighbors' trees and distributed them to people living in nearby shacks and trailers.

A Few Words About the High Desert Catholic Worker

We held monthly peace vigils at Mohave's Edwards Air force Base and we regularly joined in the prayer life of the Abbey.

Serving as the HDCW volunteer facilitator for six years, I published a newspaper, *Locusts and Wild Honey*, mailing it locally and nationally to almost a thousand readers. Once a year, a group of us trekked out into the arid desert landscape to pick the fruit off of Prickly Pear cacti, and then using a church kitchen, we cooked and canned what became famously known as Catholic Worker Cactus Jelly. Individuals and churches would offer donations in exchange for our jars of jelly.

The High Desert Catholic Worker remains a sister house of the Los Angeles Catholic Worker. When I moved back to the California Central Coast, a new Manna House was set up in Apple Valley, facilitated by Steve and Anne Bremser, who along with the Holy Spirit, keep the High Desert Catholic Worker ministries flowing out into the desert.

The Salvation Army Homeless Project

Outreach and Case Management Services, 1988–1994

A Service of The Salvation Army, San Luis Obispo CA
Captains Ed and Beryl Pearce
Toni Flynn, Coordinator, Case Management and Outreach Services
Tory Blue, Case Management and Outreach Services

Sometimes dreams actualize. The Salvation Army Homeless Project was one of those dreams come true. Captains Ed and Beryl Pearce had some County money to spend on serving the needs of the poor in San Luis Obispo. Tory and I were already Salvation Army employees and we were entrusted with the task of creating and developing a service that would really make a difference in the lives of our homeless neighbors.

With my background in Catholic Worker ministries, and Tory's experience with managing a shelter, we were a team to be reckoned with!

In no time, with the blessing of Ed and Beryl, we had set up a space in the front office of the "Sally" where folks could come in each morning to eat donuts and fruit, sip on coffee and read the local newspaper. Soon, we added two days a week of outreach, meaning we would go out into city alleys, vacant lots, creek beds, parks and street corners to visit with the homeless population in their territory. We made no demands. We always brought along clean socks, toiletries and snack items and frequently returned happily empty handed.

Our friend, Tom Beem, from County Mental Health Services would regularly accompany us on our outreach days, and while Tory and I interacted with unemployed men and women and those afflicted with alcoholism, drug addiction or milder forms of mental illness, Tom would keep busy assessing those who were burdened with grave psychiatric illnesses and those needing medical referrals.

Tom was hands down, the best problem solver I've ever worked with. He was in the system and he knew how to navigate the most vulnerable in the homeless community through all the twists and turns of every agency in town and how to convince doctors, lawyers and other professionals to assist in alleviating their suffering. He always had my and Tory's back and taught us how to avoid dead-end outcomes. On the occasions when we couldn't avoid knocking our heads silly against the proverbial brick wall, he taught us how to accept defeat and try new ways to meet our clients' needs.

During the other three days of our five-day workweek, Tory and I would see people in our office, on a drop-in basis, who wanted more in-depth guidance. We would listen to each person's story, and if they requested it, we would sign them up for case management services, thereafter meeting with them on a long-term, regular basis. We helped those on our case management list to find their way to facilities and programs offering medical, psychiatric, housing, clothing, food and housing assistance. They had access to our telephone and they could use our address to receive mail. Most importantly, if they consented, we guided them through the confusing maze of red tape involved in obtaining government services and benefits. The homeless community had a saying about us, "Toni and Tory know how to dance the Bureaucratic Boogie."

The truth is, we weren't the best of dancers. Tory and I stepped on toes and the toes didn't like it. We often, behind closed doors, threw our hands up in frustration, becoming self-righteously indignant toward many of the 'helping' agencies that never seemed to fully address the needs of the homeless population. We often felt defeated when we couldn't waltz our clients through doors that might have alleviated their problems.

Tory and I were better at refraining from judging homeless folks with whom we spent most of our days. Even when they frustrated us and even when they messed up, we never lost sight of their humanity. And as we began to learn more and more about their personal histories and current circumstances, we came to admire their ability to endure hard times and withstand the distain of many people in the larger community.

After several years, new Captains replaced the Pearce's, the original grant money dried up and the Project closed down. It was the homeless community who gave Tory and I a going away party! Fortunately, Tom Beem was able to continue with homeless outreach for many more years and was provided with a collaborative team of people from County Mental Health Services and, Transitions, a non-profit agency.

In time, new money was obtained to build a permanent homeless shelter, a day center, and a soup kitchen on the edge of town. And the San Luis Obispo Salvation Army Homeless Project, though closed, became a model for other Salvation Army sites. Tory and I, to this day, feel blessed to have known Captains Ed and Beryl Pearce and to have encountered so many unforgettable men, women and children in the homeless community.

Roy Bourgeois and the SOA

*Information compiled by Toni Flynn
and approved by Roy Bourgeois*

Born and raised in the Louisiana Bayoulands, Roy Bourgeois, a former Maryknoll Missionary, now a laicized Catholic priest, began to see the dark side of militarism while he was a Navy officer during the Vietnam War and encountered a blind Vietnamese orphan. He has since that time championed the plight of oppressed people, especially those in violent-ridden areas of Latin America including Bolivia, El Salvador, Nicaragua and Columbia. While touring and ministering in these and other Latin American countries—often at the risk of his own life—he began to observe how U.S. government policies and CIA activity aligned with powerful dictators and generals to assure U.S. corporate, economical and political advantages. And he saw how this contributed to the suffering of Latin America's poor, uneducated populations, and those who defend and assist them.

In 1980 three Catholic nuns and a lay missionary, two of whom were friends of Roy, were raped and killed in El Salvador and Archbishop Oscar Romero was assassinated. Nine years later, again in El Salvador, six Jesuit priests, along with a staff woman and her daughter, were brutally massacred. When Roy discovered links between these tragic events and graduates of the U.S. tax funded School of the Americas, located at Fort Benning in Columbus, Georgia, he became an outspoken critic of U.S. Latin American policy and the SOA. He rented an apartment in Columbus near the entrance to the school, christening it "Casa Romero".

Roy also founded the SOAWatch, a non-violent organization that is instrumental in exposing how, over the years, the SOA (now called the Western Hemisphere Institute for Security Cooperation (WHINSEC) has trained over 64,000 Latin American soldiers and officers in counterinsurgency, sniper techniques, combat, commando and psychological warfare, military intelligence and interrogation tactics. Many of the graduates return to their home countries and inflict the cruelty of what they have learned on their own people.

From 1987 until 1991 the SOA used U. S. Army and CIA interrogation manuals—now declassified—that advocate illegal detention, coercive torture techniques, the use of blackmail, sensory deprivation, electric shock, isolation, sleep and food deprivation, threatening family members, how to manipulate intolerable environments and unbearable situations and how to carry out kidnapping and murder.

In November of 1990, the first anniversary of the Jesuit massacre, SOAWatch staged a public protest. Roy was arrested and jailed. Each year since then, non-violent individuals volunteer to trespass onto the base and many are consequently sentenced to jail time, sometimes for six months. The annual crowd of witnesses at the gate has grown over the years, with often 10,000 people gathering. Roy and the SOAWatch staff indicate that this will continue until the school is closed. Meanwhile Roy continues on as the conscience of our own and other nations, speaking truth to power, being a voice for the voiceless and advocating for human rights.

To quote Roy: *Just down the road here is a school, the School of the Americas. It's a combat school. Most of the courses revolve around what they call counter insurgency warfare. Who are the insurgents? We have to ask that question. They are the poor. They are the people in Latin America who call for reform. They are the landless peasants who are hungry. They are priests, nuns, teachers, health care providers, human rights advocates, labor organizers. They become the insurgents, falsely portrayed as El Enimigo, the Enemy. And they are the ones who are the targets of those who learn their lessons at the School of the Americas.*

Overview of Toni's Arrest, Trial, and Jails in Georgia

From notes by Jan Urban

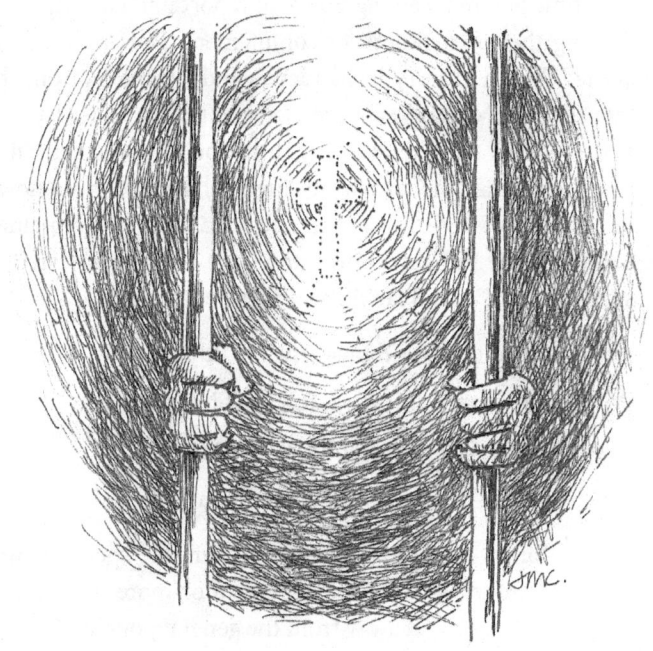

On November 18, 2001, Toni was arrested (one of 37 protestors arrested that day) during the annual SOAWatch nonviolent protest against the School of the America's, (aka WHINSEC) at Fort Benning, Georgia. She was charged with violating a 1999 'Ban and Bar'—a written order not to reenter the military property at Fort Benning for a period of five years. U.S. District Court hearing for the "SOA 37" in Columbus, Georgia. Presiding Judge was G. Mallon Faircloth; Pro Bono defense attorney was William P. Quigley. Among those present as Toni's support team were Jan Urban, Jean and Bill Basinger. Court dates were as follows: July 8, 2002, arraignment; July 9, 2002, adjudication; July 12, 2002, sentencing.

Toni was found guilty of a single misdemeanor charge of unlawfully reentering Fort Benning Military Base after receiving a previously written order in 1999 not to do so. Toni was sentenced to six months imprisonment. After sentencing, Toni and Franciscan priest, Jerry Zawada, opted to immediately begin their six-month sentences rather than return home and wait for an undesignated period of time before receiving notice to report into custody.

During their first month of confinement, Federal Marshals transported Toni and Jerry in handcuffs and leg chains from the courthouse jail to Muscogee County Jail and ten days later later, to Harris County Jail and then to their third and final destination at the Crisp County Jail in Cordele on August 1, 2002. For unknown reasons, unlike most SOA prisoners of conscience, they remained in Georgia for the full six months and were never transferred to Minimal Security Federal facilities in their home states.

- Overnight in the Columbus City Jail, July 12, 2002
- Muscogee County Jail: 2002, July 13—July 22
- Harris County Jail: 2002, July 23—July 31
- Crisp County Jail: 2002, August 1—January 9, 2003

While Toni was in the Crisp County Jail, she spent the first two weeks in a dorm-like cell that held 20 or more women at a time. She was then moved away from the general population—apparently because she was a Federal prisoner—to a lockdown cell for two (see diagram on page 27). Serendipitously, Jerry Zawada was housed next door to her.

Glimpses of Life in a Southern Jail Cell

*Crisp Co. Jail, Day 106 of 182 days,
October 26, 2002*

7:00 AM: Another morning of life in jail. Breakfast digested. Orange jumper zipped up. Clean white socks. Freshly brushed teeth. I'm locked in here with only one cellmate and, much to my dismay, an occasional water bug or field mouse.

My cellmate's name is Kaya. For reasons not clear to either of us, we are both doing lockdown time, meaning we are housed separately from the general population and rarely leave our cell. Maybe it's because I am from California and a Federal prisoner and Kaya, originally from New York, has Multiple Sclerosis. Or because our respective trials were highly publicized. Kaya is a young Black woman and I am an older white woman so it's not about racial segregation. It's crazy making trying to figure out reasons why we are in lockdown. There's very little rhyme or reason made known to inmates about the inner workings of prison systems. So, who knows? It's anyone's guess.

I've surmised that most of the regular inmates are serving sentences related to drug and alcohol offenses—dealing drugs, using drugs, forging checks for a boyfriend who is using drugs, driving drunk, setting a house on fire while under the influence of meth. When the inmates from the local region were little kids and teenagers, they went to school with other little kids and teenagers who are now either overseas serving in the military, down the road laboring in the auto parts factory, plucking chickens in the chicken factory, or right here working as correctional officers—wearing badges and holding keys and wielding power over their former classmates. Some mornings, Kaya and I peek out at the guards and the inmates through the medication flap next to our door as they march to and fro along the corridor, going to this place and that place and back again.

7:30 AM: Medication Call. A hand, masked in a surgical glove, pushes its way through the flap and drop kicks my little blue thyroid pill into my palm. I swallow it with water and sit down on my bunk. Ours is a tiny room with a common area called a day room, and two sleeping cubicles. In the common area, there's a pay phone, a metal table, two metal stools, a shower stall, an extra toilet and, mounted on the wall, a television. We each have a toilet and a sink in our sleeping cubicles. There's a thin mattress on each bunk. A plastic cup on the sink. Toilet paper next to the toilet. A small metal desk upon which I keep my transister radio, earphones, books, and mail. A storage box for keeping things like underwear and the snacks we purchase each week from commissary.

That's about the sum total of what we're allotted here. No complaints. It could be worse. For weeks, it *was* worse in the overcrowded and unsanitary cellblock where I was confined before being moved in here. In the larger unit, each of the 15 to 20 women fought to secure one of the 12 beds so they wouldn't have to sleep on the floor. They clashed over issues like the use of a single toilet where, once victoriously claimed, a person had to sit and do business fully exposed, without benefit of a privacy curtain (someone coming down from drugs tore it off and it was never replaced).

8:00 AM: Just finished following along with Denise Austin's televised 'light' workout (emphasis on 'light' for me!). I'm face up on my bunk now, head dangling over the side, hair brushing the concrete floor, arms loosely floating above my shoulders, back and bottom secure on the bunk, legs and feet stretching upward along the wall, reaching toward the ceiling. A partial shoulder stand, if you give liberties to the definition.

Glimpses of Life in a Southern Jail Cell

Kaya is in the day room watching a Soap on T.V. I hate Soaps. Still in a mock shoulder stand position on my bunk, I place my walkman headphones on, tuning into the Public Radio station. Someone's playing a solo cello piece. Deep intonations. Melancholy sounds. I wish I knew the names of the composer and composition.

I get up off of my bunk. No view from my narrow window today. Mist. Heavy mist. Everything outside—and within the regions of my head—is enveloped in an opaque and milky mystery. A veiled moment of timelessness. I once heard an Irishman in a Dublin pub refer to some foggy nights that lasted beyond anything on the clock. Maybe he had done time behind bars. Or maybe he was familiar with living in Celtic thin places, between here and there, this and that. Jail is definitely a thin place for me.

9:00 AM: Sorting through my mail. Piles of letters. I've forwarded hundreds of them back home already and have accumulated a couple of hundred more. About 80 are as yet unanswered. I've committed myself to reading and answering all of my mail, if only to scribble a few lines expressing my gratitude. Most days, I sense the presence of a loving God. Even if I didn't believe in God, I'd certainly be in the midst of a major conversion experience because of the amazing amount of supportive letters I'm receiving. So many people—strangers, acquaintances, friends, family, sending word to me. Messages like "Courage, sister, you do not walk alone . . ." and "You are not forgotten."

People write that my jail time has helped bring to their attention the need to close down the School of the Americas. Hearing about me and Jerry (my friend and fellow SOA Prisoner of Conscience who is housed next door) being detained in Georgia rather than being sent to our home States to serve our time, has prompted many supporters to question other justice issues as well. Or so the letters convey.

Arranging the letters in bundles is a favorite pastime. First, the 'Family & Friends' stack It's a mile high. Next, the stack labeled 'Catholic Nuns'. Included in that stack are cards from nuns who taught me in elementary school and high school. Another pile is the 'Strangers' stack. Letters from all over the globe written by people I've never met! Australia, all parts of the US, Canada, Germany, England, Ireland, Guatemala. Did I ever imagine having these connections?

One unusually animated letter is from an Irish hermit nun living alone in a thatched cottage on a hill in County Leitrim. She is praying for me. Two letters from a pig farmer in Iowa who says she herself is contemplating crossing the line next year at the SOA protest. Cards from a high school teacher in Wisconsin. A note in Spanish from a *compañero* in Guatemala. A set of crayon pictures from First Graders at a Catholic School somewhere in California. One young girl—daughter of a woman friend of mine—sent me a hand made paper doll with a personally designed and hand cut paper wardrobe. The human family. The Body of Christ. Filling this jail cell. This 12 foot by 12 foot walled slab of concrete.

11:00 AM: Just the two of us walking around and around in the courtyard. Kaya and I are rarely allowed time out of doors because doing so requires the accompaniment of a guard. The courtyard is dreary. Black top. Barbed wire fencing. Two broken hoops. A flat basketball. I am spending my time looking up at the sky. The fog is tickling my face. I know from the morning radio newscast that President George W. Bush is bent on dropping bombs in Iraq. I pull out my plastic prayer beads. I'm praying a rosary for peace, fingering the beads intently, as if the rotations and prayerful repetitions might really help prevent a war.

Prayer is the only peacemaking I can offer from jail. That, and the loss of my freedom. The voluntary surrender of my body for the sake of . . . what? The larger community? Justice? A better world? A fool's dream? One's purpose isn't as clear when locked away and doing time. Still and all, reciting prayers for peace on earth can't hurt. I relish knowing that all those nuns who write are praying for me too! I can almost visualize Sr. Clare Julian in solitude, praying inside her hermitage cottage in Ireland, situated atop a green hill, overlooking pastoral valleys that are perhaps covered with mist much like this . . .

Back to the cell.

Glimpses of Life in a Southern Jail Cell

12 Noon: *The Angel of the Lord declared unto Mary* . . . Lunch is a drag. Colorless processed cheese slapped between two pieces of gooey white bread. I open up the sandwich. No mayonnaise. What's on the cheese? Is that mold? Pretend it's pickle relish says Kaya. My imagination cannot expand that far. I toss the cheese and bite into the bread. No canned fruit cocktail today. I take a another bite of bread, pondering on the consequences of saying "yes" to God. *Be it done unto me according to Thy word* . . .

2:00 PM: Lying on my bunk. Reading Marianne Elliott's *The Catholics of Ulster*, reflecting on the noble (though violent) heroics of mythic Cu'Chulainn who, while suffering from a fatal wound inflicted on him by his enemies, ordered his men to tie him upright to a pillar so as to meet his death standing tall rather than on his knees.

Further thoughts running rampant through my head. I can't comprehend the root causes and effects of long-term oppression. What composes the nature of an oppressor? What about their children and their children's children? Are they inheritors of the job of being an oppressor? What about those who are oppressed? For how long does turning the other cheek make sense? What finally sets in that compels an oppressed people to rise up and retaliate? What about their heirs? What do they do with such wounds, passed on for generations? Are we humans compelled to become what most harms us? To perpetuate violence? Sometimes I am overwhelmed with my own ignorance. Sometimes, I know that I know nothing. Other times, I hope . . .

Perhaps I'm naive to embrace notions of pacifism and Redemptive Suffering. It's just that I cannot come to believe that violence leads to Resurrection and I so want to believe that *something* leads to Resurrection. My Catholic education informs me that following Jesus leads to Resurrection and that Jesus never included inciting armies along the way. Jesus was arrested and became a prisoner of conscience because he spoke truth those in authority, healed the sick on the Sabbath and lived "the better world". He hung on a Cross and forgave those who put him there. In the tomb, something happened. A refusal to stay dead. Resurrection. Julia

Each Other's Angels

Esquivel says, "Because you can't kill death with death, sow life and kill death... Sow life with life since life, as in love, is stronger than death." I find a profound and wonderful mystery in that counsel.

3:30 PM: Still on my bunk. Still reading *The Catholics of Ulster*. Acknowledging my own contradictions of character. I don't know how easily I would embrace non-violence if faced with, say, the Troubles in Northern Ireland. Many Protestants and Catholics in Belfast and Derry adhere to the 'eye for an eye' mentality of old. Each side, so sure of being 'right'. For many Irish Catholics, each new wound fuses with those of their ancestors and their rage joins the rage of centuries under British rule. I myself have a few Irish Catholic friends in Derry and Dublin who have found ways to resist current injustices without resorting to violence. Might they not be the bravest? Or at least as commendable as the romanticized warrior, Cu'Chulainn?

If put directly to the test, I wonder for how long I would endure extreme suffering, personal violation, years of internment, harm done to my family? For how long hunger, cold, poverty, loss of employment and property? For how long be forbidden to speak my mother tongue and practice the religion of my choice? For how long before striking back violently? Five minutes? Days? Years? A lifetime? These are unsettling and ironic questions to be asking from such a powerless position as I now find myself in. Better to ask, can I endure six months in a Southern jail?

4:00 PM : Late afternoon. The mist has dissipated. The sun casts long shadows. I pull myself away from the constricted window view and step into my shower stall. I shampoo my hair and wash off the musty odor of confinement. The water pours out of the nozzle in unpredictable spasms. The regulation of the water's temperature is even more haphazard. First icy cold. Then scalding hot. Jail showers are not about comfort. For that matter, neither are jail cells, jail bunks, jail meals, jail *time*.

5:00 PM: Another "B&B" dinner. My cellmate and I refer to the sorry fact that everything on our plate is either beige or brown. Brown beans. Beige potatoes. Brown gravy. Beige biscuits. And the customary slice of a questionable and unidentifiable rubbery substance. If you cut into it you discover shades of both brown and beige. Kaya calls it 'mystery meat'. I've decided it's fake food composed of shredded erasers. We don't eat it. Ever.

Somewhere beyond our locked doors, in houses with kitchens and stoves and dining tables, people are no doubt enjoying colorful food. Red tomatoes, orange carrots, collard greens, yellow corn, ruby grapefruit, golden yams, and purple cabbage. Maybe even strawberry ice cream. Not us. We're subjected to a "B&B" dinner swallowed down with a glass of murky liquid that the food servers call 'iced tea', though ice is never included.

8:00 PM: Floor mopping done by Toni. Toilets scrubbed by Kaya. Back on my bunk, headphones over my ears, tuning my Walkman on to the public radio station again (thank God for *that* comfort!). Irish music. A lament. The sound of a far-off tin whistle. I wonder . . . does the hermit nun in County Leitrim ever accept a visitor? Probably not if she's a real hermit. Still, I'd love to be on her Irish hill right now, looking over the valleys.

I'm growing homesick for my family. My tiny new grandson, Andrew James, has been breathing air, sleeping, eating, and crying for all of a week now and I've not laid eyes on him in person, let alone held him in my arms. His picture is glued to my wall with toothpaste. I gaze at his image. The tin whistle haunts my ears. I'm 3,000 miles from home.

10:00 PM: My cellmate is watching *Fox News Live* on TV. My back is to the TV but I can't avoid overhearing the reports. Talk of snipers on the streets. A commercial promoting the soothing effects of sleeping pills. Warnings of preemptive war making against Iraq. Another commercial proclaiming the luxurious rewards of owning and driving a Lexus. Is there a connection here, folks? I ask this of the walls. No reply. Somebody down at the end of the hallway begins screaming. Somebody else is banging a cup against their metal door. I think I hear Jerry's cellmate snoring next door. The walls remain mute.

11:00 PM: The lights are lowering electronically (they're never turned off). TV is mercifully turned off for the night. I'm on my bunk. Covering myself with my thin, hole-ridden coverlet.

Each Other's Angels

The only one issued me upon my arrival months ago. My jump suit serves as a pillow. My long johns as pajamas. I'm trying not to think about wake up call and the predictable cold eggs and lumpy grits of tomorrow's 6 AM breakfast.

A guard enters—I pretend to sleep. She flashes a light in my face and exits. The metal door clangs shut and her key turns. Locked inside my sleep cubicle. I'll pray for her. I'll pray for my cellmate, Kaya. For all prisoners. For the sheriff. The guards. The hog farmer in Iowa. The teacher in Wisconsin. The Irish hermit nun. My children. My grandson. My friends and other family members. I'll pray for the people of Iraq. For the President. For the military. For Irish Catholics and Irish Protestants. I'll pray for the whole wide wounded lot of us.

Perhaps tomorrow I'll chat with Jerry through the air vent we share and read the Sunday Gospel with him. Maybe Jesus will have words of encouragement for us. But that's hours from now and the hours in here move much much slower than they do in the outside world. I close my eyes and wait for sleep.

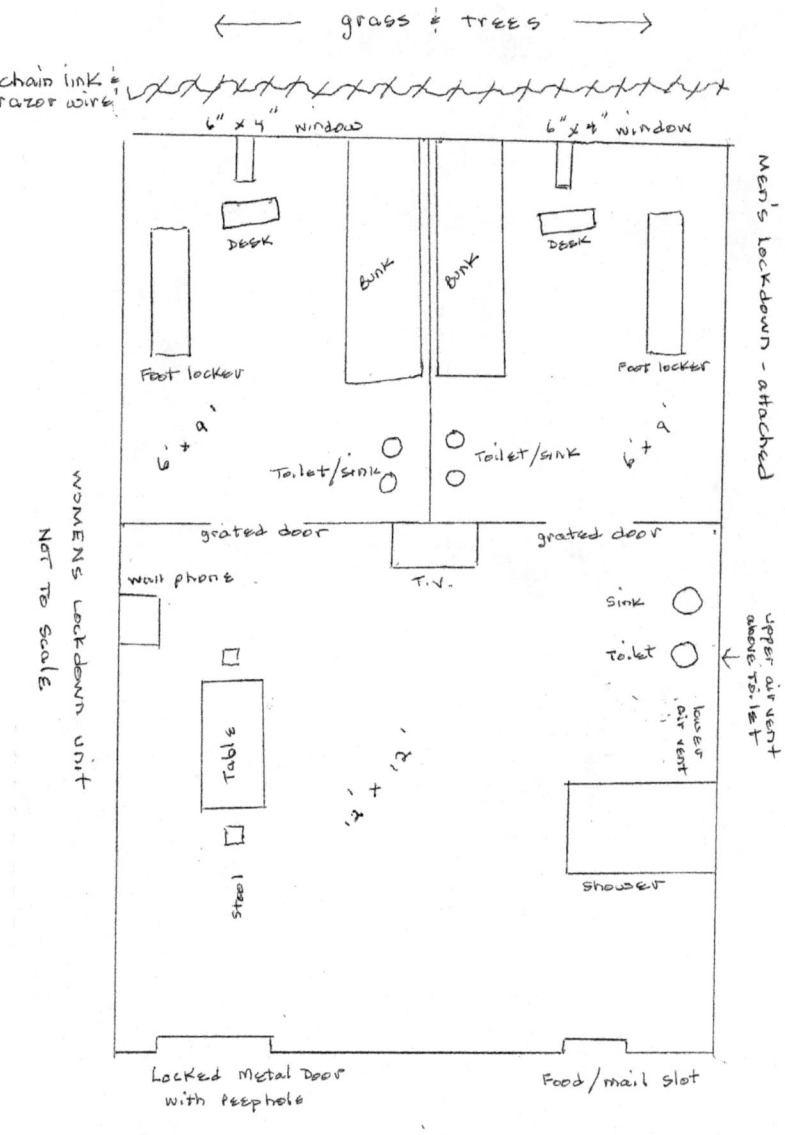

PART II

The Essays

CHAPTER 1

The Mean Streets and the Desert

Fly on, fly on past the speed of sound. I'd rather see you up than see you down . . . I will still remember Angel flying too close to the ground.

—Willie Nelson, *Angel Flying Too Close To the Ground*

A Guy Named Joe

The Salvation Army Homeless Project, 1992

It was Advent, that sacred time that invites us to slow down and patiently hold to all that is difficult, and yet I was in a rush. Gulping down a cup of steaming coffee with cream, I ran out of my office at the San Luis Obispo Salvation Army and hopped inside my car. It was time to drive over to KCBX public radio station and collect an assortment of donated Christmas cards, stamped envelopes and warm jackets, kindness of the radio staff and listeners.

Next destination was the Old Mission Catholic Church in the center of town. On my way, I noticed that several stores were opening early. No doubt it was to lure anxious shoppers—pressured by the heavily advertised annual countdown of Shopping Days before Christmas—inside to hunt for the lowest priced sales and purchase the best gifts. I took a deep breath realizing that I too had been hurrying and scurrying all morning.

As I walked up the steps of the Old Mission and over to the picnic tables on the covered porch, carrying a bundle of jackets and a bag of cards, I recognized about a dozen familiar faces among the small gathering of homeless men and women eating sandwiches. I waved. They waved back. This was the place where I regularly met up with them ever since the parish pastor had informed the city that homeless people would be welcome to eat on the porch until a decent soup kitchen was built.

I went about handing out the jackets that I had only yesterday promised to bring and then I went over to a table and spread out the Christmas cards along with some pens. Most already knew I would be bringing the cards and about half of the crowd came over, selected a card and began writing. This would most likely be the only opportunity any of them would have to send a message to loved ones. *Dear Mom . . . Dear Grandpa . . .* some told me that they hadn't contacted their family members for years. As I strolled around, I noticed that the notes didn't contain the bleaker details of their daily struggles to survive on the streets. Rather they wrote

The Mean Streets and the Desert

things like *I miss you . . . I saw a nice sunset yesterday . . . have a Merry Christmas.*

One man kept pacing up and down the porch, repeatedly passing the Christmas card table. I asked him if he would like to join us and send a card to someone. *NO!* He yelled so loud that a couple of the women shuddered, possibly fearing he would act out, pound his fist on the table, break a chair or worse. But he voluntarily backed off, leaning against a wall at the far end of the porch. Only when the last writer had addressed an envelope, sealed his card inside it and left the porch, did the man return. Lanky and tall, dressed in dirty jeans and a faded blue shirt, he sat himself down quietly at the table. He must have been in his mid-thirties, with sternly knit eyebrows and a full head of course brown hair.

"My name is Joe. Here's the thing. I can't read. I don't know how to write anything but my name." Flames of crimson shame spread across his face. I guessed that he might have come close to forfeiting the last vestiges of self-respect in that admission. After a long pause, he went on to tell me that he had been expelled from school at a young age and had worked as a day laborer for years until he broke his back in a car accident. It was impossible for him to fill out employment applications and just as impossible for him to write the information needed to receive unemployment. He confessed that he had become homeless mainly because he had been too proud to reveal to anyone that he was, in fact, illiterate.

But Joe had a desire that trumped his pride. He wanted to send a Christmas message to each of his two young daughters who lived with their mother in North Carolina. He kept their address in his wallet. And he asked if I would write something to them. "Maybe we could team up and do it together," I suggested, and further explained that he could talk out loud to his children as though they were right here, I would write everything he said onto the card and he could sign his name himself.

And so we collaborated. And Advent deepened. He said, "Thank you, ma'am." I said "Thank you right back!" And after mailing the stack of cards, including his, I drove home trusting that in about three days, two little girls would get a Christmas card from their daddy telling them that he was OK and saying how much he loved and missed them. That night, I prayed that soon Joe's sense of dignity would be restored and that he could hold to what is difficult until better times came his way. And I prayed that the message sung long ago to shepherds on a hill would one of these days be fully actualized.

Glory to God in the highest and on earth, peace and goodwill to all people.
—Luke 2:14

A Woman of No Importance

Skid Row, Los Angeles, 2003

In 1999, the Catholic Archbishop of Los Angeles was about a year into the process of building a post-modern, multi-million dollar downtown cathedral—an endeavor that would span years and cost a total of $189.7 million dollars to complete. Also in 1999, a woman of no importance had begun inhabiting a discarded refrigerator box taped to another box of no value on a Skid Row sidewalk near the Catholic Worker soup kitchen, aptly referred to by the people on the Row as the Hippie Kitchen (think volunteers in blue jeans, t-shirts and sandals).

    I met the woman of no importance on a day during that same year while taking a break from washing dishes at the Kitchen where volunteers had just served over 900 meals to those who live on the streets and in cheap Skid Row hotels. She was sitting cross-legged on the sidewalk at the entrance to her cardboard church. I say 'church' because she had somehow managed to tape the boxes together into a makeshift unit and top it off with a wooden cross above the open entryway. The woman was dressed in rags with grime from the gritty streets coating her weather worn face, neck and arms. Her graying hair was a tangled, filthy mess. However, the gentle shine in her soulful eyes reached mine as she waved a hand in my direction, indicating that I would be welcome inside.

And so I followed her inside the cardboard church, on my knees because the box was not high enough for me to stand. The cement floor beneath the thin cardboard felt cold and unforgiving. Nonetheless, I sensed the sacredness of the space. The woman of no importance knelt down in front of me, reached for and opened a cigar box, much like a priest would open a tabernacle. One by one she silently purveyed the treasures contained inside—a child-sized chipped teacup, several discarded bottle caps, a cracked compact mirror, a cheap and tarnished ruby-like clip earring.

There was no bread, no wine, but to me, the whole scene that began unfolding felt profoundly Eucharistic in quality. The woman clasped the empty teacup and reverently elevated it before me. *Holy, holy, holy,* she solemnly whispered. I felt my face flush and I was compelled to bow my head as she gently handed me what had become a blessing cup. Next she held up the earring. *Holy, holy, holy*, she prayed again as she placed the piece of costume jewelry in my lap.

As quickly as she had begun her liturgy, the woman of no importance ended it by placing the hinged lid over the cigar box, curling up in a corner, wrapping herself in newspapers, and falling into a deep sleep. Eyes closed, the sports page of the L.A. Times covering her shoulders, she noisily breathed air in and out through her half opened mouth. She had neither asked me to leave nor invited me to stay. I waited for few minutes before setting the tokens the woman had handed me on top of the cigar box, crawling out of the cardboard church, and making my way back inside the Hippie Kitchen, aware that I had just participated in a celebration that was both meek and deeply mystical.

In 2002, the magnificent three hundred, thirty-three foot long Cathedral of Our Lady of the Angels opened its massive bronze doors to the Catholic faithful and the general public, much to the chagrin of the L.A.C.W. community members who had actively protested the construction of the Cathedral, deeming it a product of the Archbishop's ambitious power; a symbol of Church affluence in a city that often neglects the poorest of the poor; an elaborate and excessively costly project, especially when at least one other option—the refurbishing of a large existing downtown church—could have resulted in a fine cathedral at a fraction of the cost. Sadly, at some point before 2002, the cardboard church, measuring approximately sixty inches wide by seventy-two inches long had disappeared from the Skid Row sidewalk along with its obscure and holy occupant, the woman of no importance.

I've never opted to visit the Cathedral, now a central feature of downtown L.A., although I've seen impressive pictures and read detailed, descriptive information flyers. And I've heard from acquaintances that it's interior is artistically and architecturally stunning. The main floor, with it's enormously high ceilings is adorned with rich tapestries, marvelous modern statuary, a massive wine-colored marble altar, a forty-two ton pipe organ, twenty four feet above the main floor, with 6,019 pipes. On a lower floor, a lavish mausoleum is exquisitely designed wherein, for a price, loved ones can be laid to rest alongside movie stars and elites of the Church in a crypt or a niche, and family members can wander through marble hallways embellished with religious ornaments, opulent lights and stained glass windows.

To this day, whenever visiting Los Angeles, I almost always avoid the popular areas of downtown, preferring the corner of Sixth and Gladys on Skid Row where volunteers at the Hippie Kitchen still lovingly prepare delicious meals, served with a smile to poor and homeless folks who can dine with dignity in a modest garden setting. The last time I was there, people were sitting at the garden tables eating steaming bowls of chicken and rice. Someone inside was tickling the ivories of an old piano, singing a sweet old-fashioned tune in a voice that intonated all are welcome and yes, important.

The Mean Streets and the Desert

Alan: Food and Company

San Luis Obispo, California

It was 1991, a year of stilted bereavement. A dear friend of mine moved to the other side of the world, another person I loved departed for new destinations of heart, and my mother died, leaving a river of estrangement between us that I did not know how to bridge this side of her grave.

These losses joined forces with a lifetime of losses. Grief rose up and held itself hostage in my throat like a fishbone. I lost my appetite and couldn't swallow any food without feeling unbearable pain. I began to lose an excess of weight. My soul, once spacious enough for joy and promise, shriveled to the size of a pinpoint. And there I balanced precariously for what seemed like an immeasurable period of time.

Weeks passed as though they were centuries. I began a descent into depression. I took temporary leave from my job at The Salvation Army Homeless Project. At first my friends expressed concern and sympathy. Eventually, most began to scold me. "Come on now." "Eat!" "It's time to get over things." However, my good friend, Guy Rathbun, telephoned me with a different message. "Since you can't eat, maybe you can drink smoothies at Hobee's." I didn't want to leave my house but Guy showed up at my door and drove me to Hobee's before I could voice a protest. The place was often referred to as a friendlier, more upscale Denny's boasting the distinction of serving a delicious Tamale Pie Special on Thursdays. And, of course fresh fruit smoothies every day.

En route to the eatery, Guy told me the story of Alan Duncan—the man who managed the Hobee's franchise in San Luis Obispo. Alan had initially lived with his family in Northern California until he felt ready to make an excruciating decision—whether to finally come out as an openly gay man and risk losing his wife whom he considered his best friend, or whether to remain in his marriage at the expense of his identity. He chose to be true to himself. He thereafter endured the anguish of a divorce followed by the shock and unbearable pain of his son's untimely death. In a similar fashion to my own response to personal loss, Alan became incapable of digesting the bitter pill of grief. Like me, he stopped eating. He stopped working.

Devastated and isolated within the realm of his sorrow, Alan sought refuge in a local Hobee's restaurant. As Guy related it, Alan would sit at a table, alone, grasping his cup of coffee as though it held all the pieces of his broken life. The waiters and waitresses took him under their wing. They became his only friends. They never suggested he purchase a meal or come to terms with his circumstances. Instead, they poured out compassion along with refills of coffee.

Over time, Alan began to order food and his heart began to mend. He vowed to move to a new city and open up a Hobee's restaurant of his own. He wanted to offer others the very things that had been served to him along side his cups of coffee—warmth, caring, and a place to heal. According to Guy, that's just what happened. Alan moved to San Luis Obispo and opened Hobee's.

Guy escorted me inside the restaurant where we were greeted by a gentle looking, soft spoken man. I immediately guessed him to be Alan. "How do you do?" he asked as he graciously took my hand and actually bowed, looking and sounding a bit like Ashley Wilkes upon meeting Scarlett O'Hara. *How do I do? How do I do? I do weakly and wearily, mournfully and morbidly.* Alan sat us at a window table and I suspected that he could read the sadness in my eyes.

Guy ordered coffee. "Toni will you have a smoothie?" "Strawberry and banana please", I whimpered. Alan studied my face. "Perhaps you'd like a little protein powder with that?" I knew that my weakness was showing, like the wilted hem of a slip below a skirt and I blushed. Alan just smiled politely. It took some time but I drank all of the protein fortified strawberry–banana concoction that he prepared for me.

I started going to Hobee's every day, ordering and drinking smoothies, sitting for minutes or hours, depending on how well I could swallow. Alan would go out of his way to greet me and over time we became friends. Not that we ever discussed private details of our lives with each other. Perhaps Guy had told Alan my story just as he had told me Alan's. Either way, it didn't seem to matter. Much like grace, our friendship was the sort of gift that didn't involve completing an information sheet or signing on the dotted line before receiving it.

It took a year before the grief in me began to subside allowing a space for healing. Still, I continued going to Hobee's, drinking smoothies and chatting with Alan. Sometimes we would talk about Broadway show tunes that we both liked. Once when we were confessing our mutual passion for the music from *Phantom of the Opera,* I decided on a whim to order a hot meal from the menu—namely the Thursday special, Tamale Pie.

My appetite for food and life returned and years rolled by like rosary beads through fingers. My mother's death, the distancing of my friend, the memory of love, all was anointed with the balm of time. Though less frequently, I would return at intervals to eat at Hobee's and to enjoy Alan's warm and caring ways. One day, he announced his plans to retire. I gave him a hug and told him I would miss him terribly and thanked him for making a difference in my life. I think he was both a bit embarrassed and pleased.

That was the last time I saw Alan. It still stuns me that he was murdered—robbed and killed in a hotel room while on a vacation in Las Vegas. When the news was published in the local paper, the whole town mourned Alan's death. I'll never understand why tragedy strikes some people more often than others. I don't know why Alan lost so much in his life and why he suffered such a brutal death. I only know I want to remember that once upon a time, I met a gentle man who ran a restaurant in my hometown and extended kindness and courtesy to everyone who sat at his tables. Especially, he was kind to me during a time of sadness and vulnerability.

Hobee's closed down quite a while ago. It was never the same welcoming place anyway after Alan left. I like to recall his genuine smile and the way his face was lined with the remembrance of pain and how often he wished me well as I took sanctuary at the little table by the window. Emily Dickinson wrote: *A door just opened* on a street—I, lost, was passing by—an instant width of warmth disclosed, and food and company. That just about says it all.

Angela

The Salvation Army, San Luis Obispo, California, 1990

For a few months, Angela was a regular visitor at The Salvation Army Homeless Project where I work in San Luis Obispo, CA. My friend, Tom, who does outreach for County Mental Health Services, introduced her to me one day and even before I knew much about her past, I began to affectionately consider her as a sort of soul sister, albeit, a very messed up soul sister. Maybe I felt connected to the way she fought against her own restlessness; or how, like me, she seemed to wander crooked roads between loneliness and a longing for human connection, between her past hurts, whatever they were and her hopes for the future.

One rainy day in winter, Angela knocked on The Salvation Army front door. When I opened it, she stood before me, a water-soaked waif in a thin blouse and a blood stained skirt. Behind her she had parked a shopping cart containing two frazzled little mixed terrier type dogs and a bunch of plastic bags stuffed full of who-knows-what.

"Toni! Ya gotta help me!" I brought Angela, along with the miniature mutts, into my office and wrapped them all in towels. She blurted out that she needed a sanitary pad because she was on "the curse" and added that her newly found pets needed dog food. "These here are my babies now, Ivy and Juniper." I shuddered at the thought of this young street girl trying to take care of two dogs—why, she couldn't even take care of herself!

I ushered Angela into the bathroom with the necessary supplies. I found some Milk Bone biscuits in The Salvation Army supply room for the dogs along with some dry clothes and a can of peaches for Angela. For the rest of the morning, I sat with her while she devoured the peaches and disclosed bits and pieces about her twenty-four years on earth that I hadn't yet heard about.

The Mean Streets and the Desert

According to Angela, she had some family members somewhere, but would not say exactly where. She ran away before she turned eighteen and had lived a homeless existence since that time, travelling here and there. Sometimes she ended up in various hospital wards for "nut cases" and sometimes doctors would send her off with prescription pills to calm her down and clear her head. "Once in a while I hear voices. They warn me about bad people who have microchips planted in their brains."

Angela went on to say that for all she knew, I could have a microchip, so she was going to be very worried for the rest of the day about having eaten the peaches I gave her because they could be tainted. With that disclosure out of the way, she rambled on about how every one of her boyfriends had caused her grief, how they fooled her into trusting them and then... pow! One after another, they turned mean and slapped her around until she would run away only to meet another boyfriend. And another.

Soon Angela grew quiet and began tending her 'babies', petting them while they curled up on her lap and singing improvised lullabies to them as they contentedly dozed. Eventually, the rain cleared and Angela decided it was time to move on. She took leave assuring me, "Nothing bad will happen to me or my babies because we're gonna take care of each other." I hugged her good-bye and as she rolled her shopping cart down the street with her dogs and plastic bags inside, I asked myself how Angela manages to maintain a hopeful outlook when burdened with so much fear and suspicion, so much exposure to the elements and so many hungry days?

I never saw Angela again. I learned from Tom that she had abandoned her shopping cart and left town with her dogs and a tattooed carnival barker who had arrived in a VW bus, staying only as long as the circus tents remained up in the county. Apparently they were headed in the direction of the next circus venue near the Bay Area. Months later, Tom came by The Salvation Army, solemnly informing me that he had received a phone call from the coroner's office in San Francisco. The coroner said that Tom's card was found on the body of a young indigent woman who was killed by a car on a busy downtown street as she went running into oncoming traffic trying to rescue her two little runaway dogs.

We both knew it was Angela. Tom sighed. Tears flooded my eyes. We decided to call the coroner back and see if the little dogs had been provided for because we knew Angela would want them safe. When we called, we were relieved to learn that a woman who witnessed the accident had adopted them. Still, I had lost my soul sister to the mean streets.

What a risk it is to engage with those on the margins of society. How foolish to establish a soulful bond with someone as rootless and damaged as Angela! Yet I was always heartened when recalling how incredibly strong she had been in her weaknesses, how generous she had been in her helplessness. Every time I thought about Angela, I celebrated how heroically she had lived and . . . died. May she rest in the perfect safety of God's protective Embrace.

Beggar Bowl Woman

Valyermo, California, Spring 2003

This is a portion of the California High Desert where small towns are strung out along the Pearblossom Highway much like sand pocked glass beads on a leather cord. Joshua trees, sagebrush, unusual rock formations and a vast horizon enhance the otherwise arid landscape. Temperatures rise to over a hundred degrees Fahrenheit in the summer and can drop to freezing in the winter. Other times of year bring strong winds or flash floods. It's unusual to ever see homeless people in the area—too extreme an environment.

Catholic Worker volunteers, myself included, live near St. Andrew's Abbey and one of our ministries is providing meals and bottled water to the Spanish speaking day laborers that wait each morning for work at the edge of town. Sometimes, I accompany one of the monks from the monastery when he brings provisions and visits with a few of the poor who live in shacks on the outskirts of town. But there is usually no call for homeless outreach.

The Mean Streets and the Desert

Spring lingers in the high desert but it soon gives way to the unmerciful heat of summer. As this past spring waned, the increasing waves of heat particularly worried me. The cause of my concern about the hot weather was a woman, wrapped in several filthy gray army blankets, squatting on a wooden pallet under a tree in the dusty lot next to an abandoned semi trailer cargo truck upon which someone had painted on the siding in red letters: He Saves. He Heals. He Delivers. The merchant at the gas station across the street from the lot had first pointed her out to me, saying she had arrived from "out of nowhere" about two weeks ago. The merchant told me he had dubbed her 'Beggar Bowl Woman' because she had in her possession, what looked like a chipped mixing bowl. Aside from the blankets, it seemed to be the only thing she owned.

As I made my way over to the truck, I asked myself, *Will Jesus save her? Heal her? Deliver her from destitution? Or will she have a heatstroke and die in the desert of dehydration?* This woman with her bowl . . . how on earth she had ever found her way to this barren borderland was a mystery to me but here she was and here I was, walking in her direction. When I approached, she paid little attention to me so I took a few more steps until I could see her face. The stench of her body was foul. I almost gagged. She reeked of urine and her wool blankets, caked with dried mud and feces, emanated a putrid, dank odor. Her wrinkle-ravaged cheeks and chapped lips were eclipsed by the piercing intensity of her dark eyes as they looked into mine with a go–away–don't–want–your–help–drop–you–cold stare. She wrapped her gnarly fingers around her bowl and I could see that her dirty, chipped, claw like fingernails had not been clipped for months or years even.

I paused in my steps with my arms relaxed and the palms of my hands intentionally open, hoping that the woman would sense I was not a threat and that I meant her no harm. It was then that I noticed lice weaving in and out of her matted hair. And I also saw a circle of twine hanging loosely around her neck with a vial of yellow liquid hanging from it. Because she was sitting, I found myself bending on my knees so that I was at her level, saying hello, giving her my name and asking her about the contents of the vial. She stiffened, holding the bowl tighter and I silently scolded myself for asking such a stupidly invasive question. I glanced up at the Jesus messages on the trailer, feeling awkward and useless.

I was about to take my leave when, for reasons I will never understand, the woman began to talk—a one-sided conversation, a confession of her circumstances, a verbal stream of consciousness. "People say I'm crazy. What do they know? I'm a gypsy. I travel around all alone. A long time ago I was raped in an ally by a bunch of guys. It was hell. I wanted to die. Then I figured out a clever thing. I stopped combing my hair and I started keeping my pee in a bottle around my neck. I can throw the pee into a guy's eyes if he tries to come too close. A better weapon than a knife! Now I smell so much that no man will ever touch me anyways. The bad news is truck drivers can't stand my stink so no one gives me rides anymore unless I lie down in the back of their pick-ups so they can't smell me and the cops can't see me. No seat belt and all that. That's how I got here. And that's how I'll leave."

I was stunned by her disclosures. *Jesus saves. Jesus heals. Jesus delivers.* This was my silent mantra as I walked across the street to the gas station convenience store and returned with a bag containing a banana, an orange, some corn chips and two bottles of water. The woman took the banana, the orange and the chips from the grocery sack and placed them in her bowl. Then she opened one of the water bottles and drank deeply. As she quenched her thirst, I fumbled around for words to signify how grateful I was to her for entrusting me, a stranger, with the gift of her story. Nothing I tried to say really expressed the feelings her revelations had evoked in my heart. And she seemed more interested in gulping water than in appreciating my words of gratitude.

I asked for her name but she opted not to disclose it. And she refused my offer of fresh clothes, a place to shower and sleep overnight, saying she was just fine under the tree. *Jesus saves. Jesus heals. Jesus delivers.* I repeated my mantra over and over as I left for the Catholic Worker house.

When, the next morning, I drove out to where the trailer truck was parked, bringing more food and water, the woman and her bowl had vanished. Was she taxied away at dawn in the back of a pick-up? Was she deposited on an unpaved road in another desert town, left to wander alone, vulnerable yet valiant in her ability to survive? Or had Jesus intervened? The questions went unanswered. I leaned against the trailer. The sun's rays were strong. So were my prayers for the Beggar Bowl Woman.

Bill: A Veteran With Nothing Left To Lean On

The Salvation Army Homeless Project, 1989

A soldier's things: his rifle, his boots full of rocks. And this one is for bravery and this one is for me and everything's a dollar in this box.

—Tom Waits

In early autumn of 1988, the leaves on the trees at Mitchel Park in San Luis Obispo were more plentiful than past years and boasted a variety of deep, rich hues of green. One afternoon, I stopped by the park to visit Bill and to appreciate with him the beauty of the trees. The very next morning, when I returned to bring Bill a promised jacket and a pair of socks from The Salvation Army where I worked, he was standing alone, in the middle of the park, overwhelmed with grief. The entire landscape was utterly and completely destroyed. He informed me that shortly after sunrise, a fully outfitted battalion of the Conservation Corps had felled the trees, dismantled the park's Veteran's Wall, brick by brick and hauled away the all the park benches. We had known this was going to happen but even so, it stunned us both to see the actual damage done.

Townsfolk had built the memorial Wall in 1947 to honor local World War II Veterans who were injured or killed in action. Forty-one years later, the city council, with the backing of a vocal group of neighborhood residents, voted in favor of spending $60,000 to build an elaborate entry arch at the far corner and to cover additional costs to raze the Wall, remove trees, benches and shrubs. The mayor proclaimed to the press that the homeless population was to blame because "they have taken us hostage in our own community" implying that their sleeping on the benches, drinking alcohol under the trees and leaning against the Veteran's Wall were reprehensible acts forcing the city to demolish the Wall and most of the park.

Yet, the town had no shelter as of yet and other than the park, homeless people had nowhere else to go once they ate donuts and drank morning coffee at The Salvation Army. Unless they were arrested and taken to jail or hid themselves away down in the creek beds, they had no alternative but to wander the streets. I couldn't help but note that the $60,000 spent to demolish the park and build a token entry arch would have gone a long way toward a decent shelter and day center.

Bill, with his waves of silver hair and a face ravaged by drinking and exposure to the elements, was visibly shaken by the whole situation. Where would he now lay his head at night? Where would he sit by day? I knew that he had grown children in another state who were concerned about his wellbeing but I knew as well that he would never choose to move back with them. I surmised from conversations with him that his refusal to consider this option was partly out of shame and partly because he was not ready to quit drinking. He had managed to survive in San Luis Obispo for over twenty five years on a fixed income of $300 a month without harming another soul. This was his town now.

He was a proud, stubborn and kind man. "I may be a homeless old drunk, but by God, I'm also a combat veteran of two wars. I was just a kid when the Big War broke out but I did what was asked of me and then I went to Korea when they called me again. I still have nightmares about what happened over seas in both wars. It's too awful to talk about but I'll tell you this, I earned the right to lean my back against that Wall for the rest of my days."

Bill knows and accepts me as a dedicated pacifist but when he finished speaking, I told him how much I wished, in that moment, that I were his Commanding Officer, honoring him while he stood at attention in full dress military uniform. I would pin a medal on his shirt, present him with a folded flag, promote him to the highest possible rank and salute him for courage under fire and bravery in the face of battle. "Don't compromise your values for me", Bill scolded. "I'll settle for another pair of socks". He winked at me and we both smiled, standing together, shoulder to shoulder, in the shadow of where the Veterans Wall had once been, a war protestor and a proud, grieving veteran.

Doc: Looking For Hope Beyond the Hype of the Season

The Salvation Army Homeless Project, December 1992

Once again December announces the season of seasons. Splinters of starlight startle the winter night sky and echoes of angels from long ago resound a great expectancy as steeple bells ring and choirs give melodic voice to hope. Tinseled evergreens grace living room windows and dazzling storefronts beckon to shoppers.

For me, however, it's a bleak period of the year when my energy wanes and barren feelings persist. Maybe it's because my job involves spending time with the poorest of the poor, mostly men, many of whom who are physically disabled or drunk or mentally incapacitated; who have no roof over their head; who wander the streets begging for coins, scavenging for road kill, drinking cheap wine from bottles wrapped in paper bags; who cover their dehydrated bodies with donated jeans, torn shirts, and castaway jackets.

Monday through Thursday I venture out to find them, in soup kitchens or on bus benches or under bridges or encamped along the creek beds. They tolerate me and sometimes they ask me for rides to the clinic or to the welfare office. It's a relief when Friday arrives and I can sit in the courtyard adjacent to the county jail, interviewing homeless people being released after serving time for such offenses as vagrancy or public intoxication. The guys are so much easier to interact with when they've been off the streets for a while and come out of custody sober, rested, washed and well fed.

Each Other's Angels

One particularly memorable Friday morning, a fellow walked out of the jail and introduced himself to me as 'Doc'. I didn't recognize him as a regular on the streets. His weary demeanor hinted at lost innocence and episodes of self-defeat. His face was grizzled, sunburned and leathery, harboring hollow cheekbones and melancholy eyes. We sat together at a table in silence for a moment or two and then, from his property bag, he pulled out some matches, rolling paper and stale tobacco and placed it on the table. Doc's nicotine stained fingers were trembling as he spread out a clump of shredded tobacco onto the paper, but he managed to roll it tight, licking the edges, and producing a perfect cigarette. He struck a match, put the pinched end of the cigarette between his lips, lit it and took a long, thoughtful draw.

I started a conversation with Doc, asking about his life and how I might be of service to him. His face contorted and grimaced as he labored to speak. "I ssss–stutter", he confessed, in a disturbingly fractured and halting manner. He kept tripping over consonants and vowels and seemed hopeful that I would be patient and listen. "It's tt–too hard for me tt–to tt–tell my ss–story so I'll show you." At that, he caught me by complete surprise and pulled off his t–shirt.

His chest was a relief map of reddish scar tissue; his shoulders and upper arms were embroidered with thick sickly pink threads of hardened flesh. Tears rolled down my cheeks. I couldn't help myself. Doc's stuttering all but disappeared as he told me about an afternoon when he was 5 years old. An adult—he wouldn't or couldn't reveal whether or not it was one of his parents, a sibling, or a stranger—doused him with kerosene and set him on fire with a kitchen match. "I was a tiny ball of human flame."

Someone he no longer recalls—a neighbor maybe—mercifully intervened and after that, he remembers only the smell of his own burned flesh, hospitals, bandages, skin grafts, poignant pain, scarring, ceaseless nightmares and a succession of foster homes. He said he was still a boy when he was discharged from the final hospital and sent to stay with his first set of foster parents. And that's when he began stuttering.

The Mean Streets and the Desert

By the time he reached the age of fifteen, Doc had abandoned foster care and had adopted himself over to the good keeping of Jack Daniel's Tennessee Whiskey. It became, he said, his antidote for anguish. He began wandering around from town to town, doing odd jobs, making his way through the Western United States in a futile effort to forget the trauma of his childhood. And it seems that his sidekick, J.D., was the cause of multiple incarcerations. "I been in and out of so many jails I lost count". He seemed almost proud of this accomplishment. "Every time I'm booked and then released, I prove to myself that I can survive anything."

Doc offered me the gift of one more personal disclosure. Once and only once, he loved a woman. His scars didn't seem to repulse her and she bore him a child, a son. He again reached into his property bag and pulled out a faded snapshot of a beautiful baby boy. His stutter returned as he spoke. "Of course, the picture is old and he'd be all ggg–growed up by now. Someday I'm ggg–gonna find him."

I waited while Doc pulled on his shirt and along with it, some semblance of dignity. He asked me for a ride back to town. When I dropped him off on a corner, I shook his hand and said, "I really hope you find your son." As he walked away I had a brief vision of him restored to wholeness in body and spirit, sharing a meal with his son. But he was already sauntering in the direction of the nearest liquor store, where he no doubt would use his last dollars to purchase a bottle of his best friend, Jack Daniel. I guessed he would be back in jail by Christmas Eve.

It dawned on me in that moment that maybe the Christmas Season is less for happy children and pious churchgoers than it is for wounded kids and flawed adults. Maybe it's for those of us who keep our lamps dim with doubts and depression; for those who wander, thirsting in the desert of broken dreams; for prisoners behind bars and those of us who hold our own hearts captive. Perhaps Christmas is more appropriate for the lost and lonely and disillusioned and for those of us who have, at some point in time, been blind to the light of a guiding star and failed to hear the songs of angels on high.

Each Other's Angels

I want to believe that this Christmas proves especially meaningful for Doc, who has entered and exited countless Bethlehem towns, searching for his son, reaching past horrible memories, disabling addiction, and a disfigured body toward healing. May this town shed a little good will his way and even if he's re-arrested, may the cops be kind and may invisible Hosts on High navigate him a bit closer to the Peace that Surpasses All Understanding.

Exiles in the Desert

High Desert Catholic Worker, 2001

Part I: En-Route to Mira Loma

Perhaps others can go around the desert on the simpler route . . . but the way of God's people is always through it.

—Belden C. Lane, *The Solace of Fierce Landscapes*

The late morning's summer sun mercilessly pours over the High Desert, transforming the Pearblossom Highway into a miles long frying grill. I turn on the air conditioning in my 1988 Toyota hatchback, thanking God that it still works, drive away from the shaded sanctuary of St. Andrew's Abbey where I just finished chanting Lauds with the monks, and begin the hour long drive to Lancaster for my weekly visit with the men detained at Mira Loma INS (Immigration and Naturalization Service) Center.

Cruising past Cactus Kate's Saloon where a sign invites carnivorous cowboys to a weekend pig roast, and past the Orbit where acres of junk beckon bargain hunters and seekers of lost treasure, I turn northward onto one of the numbered streets. Never having developed an innate sense of direction, it's thrilling for me to live in an area where mountains cradle the desert valley region and all of the streets running north and south are identified by numbers while those that run east and west have letters. So convenient!

The Mean Streets and the Desert

Except that this is the desert and everything here that seems convenient is only deceptively so.

In actuality, the Pearblossom Highway and many of the numbered and lettered streets, with their endlessly monotonous ribbons of scorching blacktop and single lanes devoid of passing shoulders, are the reason that this stretch of desert has earned the dreadful distinction of being dubbed the 'Head-on Collision Capital of California'. The local tourist shops make a small fortune selling silk screen t-shirts that confirm, "I survived the Pearblossom Highway". Even the locals buy them. The shirts are humorous yet morbid since many drivers and their passengers do in fact meet their death on the infamous highway. I bless myself with the Sign of the Cross each time I pass one of the numerous makeshift highway memorials adorned with hand-made crosses and plastic flowers, emblematic—to me anyway—of the interlacing of God's Divine design for humanity with our own fragility and random moments of recklessness.

Halfway to my destination, I begin my ritual of reciting the rosary for the men I will be visiting at Mira Loma. *Our Father who art in Heaven . . . Hail Mary, full of grace . . . Glory be to the Father and the Son and the Holy Ghost . . . Amen.* From regions in Mexico, Central and South America, Africa and China, many of the now detained men had carried very little more than hope on their backs, as they braved their treacherous journey to the U.S. to escape poverty, oppression and violence.

Although a few detainees are here waiting to be deported because of crimes committed on U.S. soil, numerous asylum seekers entered the United States illegally, escaping real threats of torture and death in their homelands. Those desperate men now find themselves locked away in this INS facility, tangled in a web of confusing and punitive immigration regulations and delayed deportation proceedings. Many others at Mira Loma—believing that they had arrived in the U.S. with their papers in order—settled into low wage job positions, got married, had children only to be years later rounded up by the ICE (Immigration and Customs Enforcers) and detained because of glitches in immigration law. Torn from employment and families, they live in a precarious limbo for months on end, too poor to retain decent representation, while their wives and children are left to fend for themselves.

My Toyota hatchback whirs along. I boost the air conditioning to high and turn on the radio to a desert station where Willie Nelson, the Shakespeare of Country Music, is singing something sweet and sad. Outside, long rows of water wheels defy the scorching heat and sprinkle fragile, young fields of onions and alfalfa. In the distance, mature crops are being harvested by sweating day laborers—both men and women—who bend their backs to pick and place onions into gunnysacks and bale the dried alfalfa into stacks. I pray that they are provided with water and breaks in the shade. I wonder to myself if their lives don't also add up to another harsh form of detention.

Soon the scenery is all about vacant lots of sand and tumbleweeds rolling by a few run down trailer courts with the trailers' noisy swamp coolers converting the extreme dry heat in their living spaces into cool water vapor. Then the landscape changes again as I reach the far edge of Lancaster with its rows of cheap stucco apartments, fast food joints, beer bars, coin laundries, pawn shops, used tire stores, gas stations and thirsty crows on telephone poles. Then nothing but burning, juiceless sand until suddenly, like a mirage, a massive movie theatre complex appears in the middle of practically nowhere, announcing the promise of entertainment, relief from the sun, and extra large cups of ice cold soda. The scene is surrealistic to say the least.

With only a few miles to go now, I drive on while the radio D.J warns that temperatures will reach well over 105 degrees by noon. I look at my watch. It's 11:00 am and already I imagine that it's hot enough to fry an egg on the hood of my car. At last, I arrive at Mira Loma, park my car in a space designated for volunteers, show my ID to a guard who opens two sets of gates for me. John, the Jesuit Chaplain, is waiting to escort me inside. We walk together silently through a long sidewalk corridor, barbed wire fencing on either side of us—the liminal space between freedom and captivity.

Exiles in the Desert

High Desert Catholic Worker, 2001

Part II: Inside Mira Loma

Here a new community takes shape, a community formed in brokenness, constituted on the edge . . .

—Belden C. Lane, *The Solace of Fierce Landscapes*

Afterwards, I learned that the multicultural gathering in the Catholic Chaplain's classroom at Mira Loma had been a serious mistake on the part of a new custody officer, and one that might have resulted in a riot. However, while the event was in process, I experienced it as a grace-filled sign of God's expansive compassion working through me and through the detained men. I still hold to that.

It was a sunny Sunday afternoon and Mother's Day. Chaplain John had already celebrated a bi-lingual Mass for a large Latino gathering in the chapel and we had both just finished lunch. He went to his office to hear a confession and I went next door to our classroom, prepared to give an English language lesson to about five men from Mexico who had signed up for a weekly course. But I found myself facing over forty men from a variety of countries including—Colombia, Guatemala, El Salvador, Nigeria, The People's Republic of China, and yes, Mexico. The escorting officer gave me a written list of names and countries of origin just before he walked away.

As a volunteer assistant chaplain at Mira Loma, I had learned to expect the unexpected but this situation caught me by complete surprise. What can I—who barely speaks more than a few Spanish phrases—offer this multicultural group? I had to think fast, something I'm not adept at, preferring to reflect and ponder before acting. Posing a practical question seemed best. "Does anyone here speak English?" To my profound relief, a few raised their hands. I asked those few to identify their respective countries on a wall map. One man was from Mexico, one from Guatemala, two from Nigeria, and one very young man from a province in China. Thankfully, they all agreed to join me next to the white board and serve as my interpreters.

Looking around the room, I found myself pausing and gazing at the faces of the men. It was an emotional moment as I realized that the details of their stories were mysteries to me and most likely to each other—stories that included exile and hardship, poverty and uncertainty, oppression and war, fear, hunger, narrow escapes, loss of freedom. For all I knew, in this very room, a man from one country might consider a man from another region or country to be his enemy. What might be a bonding factor, what do we have in common?

It's Mother's Day, I reminded myself, and whether our mother was living or dead, kind or unkind; whether she gave us away at birth or nurtured us into adulthood, we all had mothers. And we wouldn't be alive if our mothers had not borne us into the world. Enlightened by this thought, I explained through the interpreters that in this country, today was the day set aside each year to honor our mothers. I shared that even though my own mother had died and we had not been close, I still remembered her every Mother's Day. Approaching the extra large white board, I printed my mother's name—Julia—and I spoke her name out loud. I handed markers to the interpreters and they each wrote their mothers' names on the board—using the alphabet native to their country and saying the name out loud.

Next, I invited everyone to get in line and when their turn came, to write their mother's name or draw a symbol representing her and say her name aloud. Not a one declined the offer. Many cried. The board was filled with names and symbols. I shed some tears too, thinking about how, for one reason or another, these men had been unwillingly brought together in captivity at Mira Loma, far from their homelands, locked away with strangers, many from other cultures, separated from family, forced to wait months on end, often with no representation, pressured into signing papers they didn't fully understand, while officials determined their futures. And yet, for two hours, while wars raged on around the globe, these men were able to form a diverse and peaceful world community, honoring their mothers in this little classroom surrounded by barbed wire in the middle of a vast desert.

Fond Farewell To A Noble Friend

San Luis Obispo, 2013

As a teen, I curled my hair with empty orange juice cans, wore a Miraculous Medal on a silver chain around my neck and wrote poetry during Algebra class. Michael Thomas Horton was my classmate and best pal at St. Monica's Catholic High School in Southern California. He was a red headed, freckle faced Venice Boy who loved to surf at Sorrento Beach and wore Hawaiian shirts to Mass on Sundays.

Michael and I had families that struggled with demons. Michael was the first—and for a long time—the only friend with whom I shared confidences about the shame of growing up in an alcoholic household where money was scarce and tempers ran high. No one . . . I mean *no one* in high school dared disclose such secrets to their schoolmates. But I did to Michael. Then one day, Michael entrusted me with the traumatic story of his own childhood . . . how, soon after his father abandoned the family when Michael was a little guy of 6 years old—his mother went up to her bedroom and shot herself. He found her dead. It would have been understandable for Michael to become a haunted, violent, vengeful adult. Yet, instead, he grew into a loving husband, gentle father, compassionate neighbor, loyal friend. Quick witted and grateful for life itself, he looked for opportunities to cheer people up and extend a helping hand.

I first met Michael at a sock hop during our freshmen year. By the time we completed our senior year and marched up the aisle in caps and gowns to the tune of Pomp and Circumstance, we had seen each other through our respective teenage heartthrobs and heartbreaks and had sealed a friendship that would last longer than any of our high school romances. We kept in good touch over the decades. Eventually, we both found ourselves living with our respective families along the California Central Coast and visited often.

Michael recently died of an aggressive form of cancer. It struck him with a vengeance. It caused him pain. It killed him, robbing him of more precious time with his beloved spouse, Liz, and his awesome children. And I was denied more years enjoying the company of a guy I really loved. When I first heard the sad news from Liz, my emotional filters dissolved in grief. I missed three days of work, covering up in bed, dreaming fitful dreams. I couldn't shed a single tear. Worse, I couldn't comfort Michael's family because I could think of no way to console their complete loss.

The morning that I finally got out of bed, I drove myself to the Steaming Bean Café, and purchased three different newspapers and darkly immersed myself into the news of the day. Maybe I wanted to find news of things more insidious than cancer. And find it I did. From the front page to the back, stories unfolded like a child's night terrors, bad news, sensational news, scandalous news, violent and fear invoking news.

It was all there printed on paper in black ink: Pimps scarring prostitutes who didn't bring in enough profit; drug dealers executing dopers who ratted on them; homeless addicts dying alone in gutters; drunk drivers passing out on their way to fatal head–on collisions; jealous husbands beating wives and wives stabbing wayward husbands; policemen banging the heads of handcuffed men on cement walls; young gang members driving down inner city streets in their cars, shooting rival gang members.

On other news pages, I found featured stories of foot soldiers and airmen returning home after multiple combat deployments, trying to adjust to being legless, armless, blind and scarred. Others returning with less visible wounds unable to cope, feeling soulless, leaving suicide notes on their beds, putting guns to their heads and pulling the triggers. There were additional reports about enlisted

The Mean Streets and the Desert

men behind the controls of Predator Drones, striking various targets as though they were playing video games yet knowing that the 'collateral damage' would likely include not only civilian men but also women, pregnant mothers-to-be and innocent children.

It was masochistic of me I know, but I kept pouring through all of the news articles spread out before me, each more unbearable than the previous one until finally I wept, allowing my personal grief to mingle with the sorrows of the world. And suddenly, in an epiphanous moment, I saw the importance of rooting out the causes of suffering that lie within us and around us and replacing them with healthier thoughts and actions. So, I mailed a card to Liz offering to help plan the celebration of Michael's life at his memorial service. And I showed up at the service, along with over a hundred others, to pay homage to him. And it was a grand celebration indeed!

For a long while after that, I avoided the café and the newspapers. I often walked on the beach, my thoughts returning to earlier years when Michael and I were teens and the whole world—just prior to President Kennedy's assassination—still felt innocent, at least to to us. I smiled at the memory when one hot summer night, we subversively sneaked over a wall and under a fence and into the back lots of Desi-Lu Studio where, on contrived Western sets, we scripted, directed and acted out cowboy scenarios borrowed from the real and imagined comedies and tragedies of our own young lives.

I chuckled when recalling how Michael and I mastered the technique of 'invisibly' infiltrating the local drive-in movie theatre by walking around the back entrance barrier, our pockets stuffed with licorice sticks and Mars bars, with a great sense of accomplishment. Once in, we would set up our outdoor beach chairs under the stars and enjoy some of the best movies the early Sixties had to offer: Sean Connery morphing into James Bond in Dr. No and Goldfinger; Steve McQueen, the Cooler King, making his Great Escape; the Beatles having a Hard Day's Night.

In addition to our outdoor movie excursions, we also had fun driving out to LAX to watch planes take off and land, pretending we were passengers waiting for flights to exotic lands. And one of the best memories was that of using our investigative brilliance to outguess Basil Rathbone—as Sherlock Holmes—in solving who-done-it reruns of Sherlock Holmes on the black and white T.V. at Michael's Granny's house in Venice.

During his adult life, Michael experienced some hard times, battling alcoholism for years before finally becoming sober and committing to a Twelve-Step Program. But he possessed a remarkable sense of humor and used it, rather than his fists, to resolve conflicts and dissipate aggression. He loved his wife and kids. He was a skilled fisherman and sailor who once saved a drowning man's life at sea. He never sought recognition nor made headlines for his many triumphs over adversity and his good deeds. He simply and humbly overcame the odds that were stacked against him and made the world a better place. He was, I think, a noble man.

When I say 'noble' I mean he was a genuine person who helped others and transcended his own personal suffering. When I looked up nobility in the dictionary, to my disappointment, found that 'noble men' and 'noble women' over the centuries, have been defined by such superficial elements as inherited title, wealth, property, privilege, prestige, rare jewels, fine clothes, silk purses, Peacock feathers and snuff. Kings, queens, lords, ladies, even bishops and popes have a history of presenting themselves in specially designed wardrobes to distinguish them from the common masses, elevate them to a 'nobler' status.

In this day and age, we go ga-ga over the low-cut silver gowns and black tuxedos of movie stars, and the jeweled crowns of royalty. More disturbing and dangerous, we often exalt the self-appointed "nobles" of our era who feel entitled as a result of their tabloid celebrity, manipulative political actions, aggressive support of militarism, corporate power strategies and excessive accumulations of money and property at the expense of others.

In my dictionary, right underneath the description of 'Nobility', is the description of 'Nobody', said to mean a person of no public importance, influence or social station. I believe that truly noble men and noble women are ironically often found among the 'nobodies' who at some time in their lives understand what it means to descend into the lowest places. "A high station in life" says Tennessee Williams, "is earned by the gallantry with which appalling experiences are survived with grace". That just about sums up Michael, the noblest of 'nobodies'! A funny, gallant, kind-hearted man who I'm sure now occupies a seat of high honor in heaven.

Imagine William's World

The Salvation Army Homeless Project,
San Luis Obispo, California, 1993

Imagine that you are mentally and emotionally fractured. In some indigenous shamanistic cultures your extreme distress would be honored as a spiritual crisis. With the assistance of rituals and the support of the larger community, you would travel on an inner journey and eventually, after a long period of agony and darkness, you would break through into the light, becoming 're-born' as a healer with special gifts to offer others.

Now, imagine that you are presently homeless and seriously mentally ill on the streets of San Luis Obispo, California. Your name is William. Once you were a bright and happy little blond boy surrounded by loving mid-western family members. You aced math in fifth grade, ran track in high school, took a pretty girl to the Senior Prom, and won a scholarship to a university. Something happened, though, when you turned nineteen. You grew suspicious of people. You failed all your classes. You stopped eating. Your parents intervened. You were admitted to a psychiatric hospital and placed on a medication called Haldol. The drug made you drowsy, your legs and arms weakened, your hands trembled, your mouth felt as though it was filled with cotton. As soon as you were discharged from the hospital, you stopped taking the Haldol. And you hopped a Greyhound bus that took you as far west as you could go.

Now your thoughts are fragmented, scattered, split. You are experiencing personal anguish and absorbing the psychic shadow of modern society. Your clothes are dirty and torn and you need a bath. You feel isolated and lonely but at the same time, you can't trust another living soul. Last week, someone beat and robbed you of spare change and a tuna sandwich while you were sleeping on a bus bench after dark. This morning, a mother going into the supermarket passed you by and shielded her children from your view. About an hour ago, a couple of drug addicts tried to sell you some heroin and when you refused the offer, they spit on you and called you a 'nutcase'.

You constantly hear voices coming from out of nowhere, penetrating your skull, and filling your head with horrible messages. One voice in particular sounds like an evil echo in a cave. A whole chorus of voices taunts you at night when you huddle under a bridge after dark. It's impossible to sleep anyway with cars zooming by on the freeway above. During the day, the voices warn you to avoid meals at the soup kitchen and donuts at the day center—the food is poison they say. So you rummage through trashcans and dumpsters, handpicking pieces of discarded sandwiches and fruit. You will only drink water from a particular water fountain at a particular park. So you're thirsty a lot.

Convinced that people you see on the streets are secret enemy agents and that you are being followed by the FBI, you keep moving around town, circling city blocks, hour after hour. Every once in a while, on your rounds, certain individuals throw you a troubled glance. The voices assure you that everyone wants you dead. As if that's not enough, the voices laugh at you and tell you that Satan thinks you are a worthless joke of a man. From time to time, you mumble retorts and responses or mock their ongoing merciless chatter.

The tragic truth is that you are no longer able to distinguish the outer world from the inner world because margins and boundaries are nonexistent. The voices are a woven part of the tapestry of your life. You cannot think even a single thought through to the end without one of the voices interfering. As William, you will never know whether your psyche is hopelessly broken or whether you are a victim of a broken system where there is no room for your

The Mean Streets and the Desert

type of sensitivity and predisposition. You will find it impossible to sustain yourself in a society where persons are considered 'normal' only if they are able to exist under the conditions, pressures and pursuits that demand certain standards of success and conformity. 'Crazy' people are simply not accepted in such a society.

Now imagine for a moment that you are a person like me, working with homeless people suffering from mental illness. You leave your own house and family each morning and enter what is literally another world, incomprehensible for the most part to others in your community. You go out to the cemetery looking for William who, if he's not sleeping under a bridge often spends the night curled up on a gravestone. When you find him, you offer him a sandwich, which he refuses to take, a bottle of water, that he pours onto the cemetery lawn. For the umpteenth time, you offer to drive him to a nearby doctor who could administer a low dose of a new medication—one that would clear his mind with fewer side effects than the Haldol he once took. He runs away shaking his head, shrieking "No. No. Never again."

He's not the only one in town who shakes a head at you. The politicians, police, business owners and neighbors seem to believe that you are simply applying bandages to casualties in a bloody field. And just about every other day you see it that way too. But you gather strength. When you enter the realm of the unwashed, unacknowledged, and unaccepted, you learn a tremendous amount about human life.

The homeless, mentally anguished human beings, with whom you spend your days, challenge every value, notion, and ethic that defines you. They force you to see the human condition torn and turned inside out with knotted threads and ragged seams. And over time, you become aligned with the walking wounded of the streets and you get a sense of their poverty. Not so much the poverty of having no money and no house, although that's a pitiful part of their circumstances. What really get's you is the poverty of their alienation.

You stand next to a panhandler on a corner and watch shoppers and tourists rush by averting their eyes. You can't help but wonder why it's so offensive for us to be asked for a buck by a man in rags when a little farther down the same street, we happily accept a display ad's command to spend a part of our paycheck on the newest shade of raving red lipstick. You become increasingly aware that homeless people are easy targets to fear and condemn simply because they have no walls or automobiles to hide behind. A drunk and broken man urinating in his pants on a public sidewalk prompts as much vocal outrage as local newspaper stories about murder, rape and child abuse committed by people who live in houses.

William is sitting on a bus bench now and this time you decide to walk by and just say "Hi"—maybe gain a little trust. For a long time now, you've debated the value of trying to 'fix' people like William so that they can re-enter a society that rejects the 'unfixed'. You realize that it's time to accept the fact that William isn't ready to consider medication. He harms no one by spending his time wrapped in thin shreds of autonomy, moving around town from a gravestone to a bridge to a bus bench, drinking water from a favored fountain and eating self selected, carefully inspected food. "Peace be with you, William." You say this instead of "Hi". He nods and almost smiles and you consider this a major victory.

No organizational charts, no statistical information, no sophisticated formula for success, no amount of funding can ultimately heal a human being. When you choose to engage a person like William, you learn to respect their ability to survive in the face of unfathomable difficulties. You learn to traverse the long haul of relationship versus the quick fix of accomplishment. You begin to relinquish your inclination to control the destiny of another human life and yet you refuse to label anyone hopeless.

I have taken to imagining a better world where, without exception, everyone is in a procession toward compassion. If someone in the procession can't keep up, someone else slows things down. If someone falls, someone else lends a hand. If someone's mind or heart breaks, someone else marches with them through the brokenness. It's good to imagine this because one day I might be slow and fall and break. More importantly, it's good to imagine the sort of world where everyone, William included, enjoys God's promise of a new earth in which righteousness dwells.

Michael: Soap Box Prophet

San Luis Obispo, California

Less than a half block from the downtown Palm Theatre where I was headed on foot to see a Woody Allen film, Michael spotted me. Even though this encounter happened back in the early 90's, when I worked full time for The Salvation Army Homeless Project, I remember it well. In those days, I really looked forward to weekends as a time of rest and recuperation from my weekday immersion with the down and outs on the bitter side of town where misbegotten souls never had a day off from their situation.

Michael was barefoot, wobbling atop a milk crate on the corner nearest the movie theatre, waving his arms as though in charge of the traffic signal, dressed in his usual garb of filthy jeans and a tattered long sleeved shirt. He was ranting and raving to passing cars at the top of his lungs, a nonsensical barrage of phrases followed by bleak, catastrophic warnings of disaster. "Reeeepent! The planet is doomed! We are all damned!"

There was no way I could avoid approaching Michael unless I wanted to be late for the movie. When I got to the corner, he looked down from the poverty of his pedestal, his eyes rolling around wildly in their sockets and suddenly he focused, gazing at me with something akin to sanity. After a few seconds he said, "Hi Toni. Did you hear about me becoming a preacher? And I'm running for pope. Will you vote for me?" I was in a hurry but Michael offered me an opportunity to stop and recognize the value of having a downtown soap box prophet. I replied to him with great respect and boisterous enthusiasm. "Yes! Yes I will vote for you, Michael!" And then I moved on to keep my date with Woody Alan.

"Yes!" he yelled at a Mustang convertible. "The lady said, 'Yes!'" he screamed at a rusted Chevy pickup truck. "There's hope for the world!" he shouted to a shiny Volvo sedan. Then he proclaimed to a collection of wary pedestrians, "Everything is gonna be all right now! We are definitely saved!"

When I was near the front of the movie line, I turned to see Michael descend from his milk crate, pick it up, tuck it under his arm and shuffle down the street taking his sad history with him—stories that I knew only too well from reviewing his jail, psychiatric and medical records. I learned even more from reading the scars on his arms and legs—old cuts and cigarette burns inflicted on him during his childhood. I knew as well that he was tortured by voices and delusions of persecution, eased only by the cheap, brain cell destroying habit of whiffing Toluene fumes from brown paper bags.

People from numerous non-profit agencies—including myself—tried for years to help Michael and direct him to services for food, clothing and shelter. None of us ever succeeded. When he wasn't in jail on vagrancy charges—and he often was—he ate out of trashcans and camped in dry creek beds. When his shirts became too tattered or his jeans too full of holes, he sometimes stole clothes off of neighborhood clotheslines. His trust of others having been violated so many times when he was a youngster, he repeatedly refused all direct attempts to provide him with help and assistance as an adult.

Eventually, Michael disappeared from the downtown area. Rumor had it that he was hospitalized somewhere with a rare sort of bacterial infection wherein the outer lining of his heart began tearing apart and disintegrating. In other words, he was suffering from a broken heart. Whether that misfortune actually befell him and if so, whether he survived the ordeal is unknown to me. I know only that Michael gave me reason to pause on a street corner one day and when I gave him my 'yes' he seemed to feel a rare moment of triumph. As for me, the grace of that brief interaction lingers on inside of me and—in Michael's honor—I pull it out and give scoops of it away at every possible opportunity.

The Mean Streets and the Desert

My flesh and my heart may fail, but God is the strength of my heart and my portion forever.

—Psalm 73:26

People With Habits

Arroyo Grande, California, May, 2015

Restlessness and contradiciton are my habits. I tend to pamper them like spoiled children. Especially when it comes to figuring out whether I'm called to lead an active life versus a contemplative one. Years ago, after my children had grown, I had the unique opportunity of living through numerous seasons as a solitude, first in a cottage on Inis Mor, a secluded island just off the west coast of Ireland and later, within the cloister of La Casa de Maria Retreat Center nestled between the mountains and shorelines of coastal California. Throughout those exquisite experiences, I would sometimes pause in the midst of my solitary tasks, and wonder what it would be like to entirely immerse myself into the active, energetic spiritual dynamics of a Catholic Worker community.

After living and working at the retreat center for two years, I grew restless and prayed for guidance at great length, finally deciding to set up a Catholic Worker retreat house in the desert. To prepare myself for full time Catholic Worker life, I moved in with Helen and Curt who facilitated their Catholic Worker house in a bustling harbor town near the Port of Los Angeles. With great expectancy, I threw myself into a fever of extraordinary activity. For five months I worked long hours serving meals to hungry people, offering overnight hospitality to homeless men and women, sharing room space with other community members, distributing clothing to needy families, and holding peace signs on street corners in the company of other activists. I found myself living life wholly in service to others and doing it with just as much fervor as I had previously lived and breathed, prayed and read, written and walked in contemplative repose.

Then I grew tired. Restlessness and contradiction called on me like the old habits they are, and I answered by declaring to Helen that I needed to pull away from community and the city streets and take a monastic break. I phoned Leia, a fellow Catholic Worker in Orange County, and suggested that we go on retreat together somewhere to restore ourselves and renew our sense of mission. Leia suggested that in lieu of that idea, I visit her at Isaiah House where she resided and where we could have a "mini retreat" in a newly refurbished upstairs prayer room. I thought about it for a minute and said, "Sure. Great!"

The next Saturday, I showed up at Leia's place with lots of lofty notions and naive expectations. I charted out in my head how the two of us would devote an entire morning to seeking the Face of God, barefoot and behind the closed doors of the chapel. We would pour and drink fragrant cups of Green Tea from a steeping pot. We would read Rumi. We would perfect our Yoga postures. We would iron freshly laundered altar cloths as a form of meditation. We would consider the monastic scriptural practice of praying Lectio Divina as a vehicle to enlightenment.

"Something has come up", was how Leia put it as she greeted me on her porch. I winced. She had been called in to the local jail to meet with some of the incarcerated women. Upon invitation, I reluctantly accompanied her. We passed clearance through jail security and were escorted into a small sort of classroom where a few women inmates were already gathered. "In the name of the Father and of the Son and of the Holy Spirit . . ." Leia was ministering to the women. Helping them pray. Listening to their problems. I was silently shadow-boxing with my contradictions. *What am I doing here? OK, I'll be present and other-centered, it's only right and just. No . . . really, I'd rather be in the prayer room.* But, I wasn't. I was in the jail. So much for monasticism!

Just as my internal laments were hitting an embarrassingly low minor key, and as Leia was concluding the prayer session, one of the women approached me. She looked like a child except for her gray complexion and the dark circles under her eyes. When she spoke, her raspy voice was devoid of innocent resonances, scarred with undertones of self-defeat. She handed me a piece of scrap paper. "It's a poem. I wrote it. I thought you might like to read it." What could I do but accept the offering? I unfolded the tattered little paper and began to read the young woman's pencil written words:

> "My soul put on hold
> Just trying to keep on living.
> Trying to believe I can still be saved.
> Asking myself
> Is it too late, can I kick it
> This habit of mine?
> Love—is it powerful enough
> To conquer my deceptions?
> The river's long and getting deep.
> Hopefully I'll make it to the other side
> Of this nightmare on 'Meth Street'
> Before it's too late.
> At one time I may have been
> A good person.
> What a shame."

I read it and I re-read it. In Lectio Divina fashion, I pondered on its meaning and on how it affected me. The young woman had a habit. It was destroying her life. But it was a habit she could identify in a poem and therefore she had a chance at redemption from its death clutch. I told her this and she seemed grateful. It may sound twisted but for a moment I found myself wishing that I too were addicted to street drugs or to alcohol. As abhorrent and masochistic as that momentary wish may seem, what's behind it is the truth that drug addiction and alcoholism are namable diseases. You can palpate them. They render you visibly powerless. If you die from an overdose or from liver failure, you die of a diagnosable condition. If you embrace sobriety, your abstinence and recovery practices tell you and the community that something heroic and good is unfolding in your life.

My own emotional ailments, compulsive dysfunctions and contradictions of character are smoke screened behind the appearance of normalcy. I can smooth on my lip gloss, powder my nose and wear colorful scarves with my t-shirts. I can feed poor people. I can pray. I can stand with a peace sign on street corners. Doesn't that that say to others that I'm "OK"? Doesn't it help me face myself in the mirror? Isn't this proof that I have been spared the addiction gene that overwhelms not only the jailed poet but many of my own family members?

By the time we left the jail, the sun was setting. I tried to brush away a rising sense of vague indignation over the disturbing questions that had arisen in my mind because of the pain and pathos expressed in the young prisoner's poem. As Leia and I drove into the driveway at Isaiah house with the hope and intention of salvaging the rest of our visit and proceeding into the prayer room, I intuited that something was amiss.

There are just some days that refuse to allow you to escape confronting your own shadow and this was turning out to be one of them. Leia and I walked up the front steps and into chaos. In our absence, one of the homeless guests had smuggled alcohol into the house and practically the whole household was now falling down drunk. One guest was throwing up all over the porch. The first word out of Leia's mouth was, "What are you doing drunk in a clean and sober house?" To which the inebriated man replied in between vomiting spasms, "What do you expect? I'm an alcoholic. This is what I do best." Only a couple of guests had refrained from drinking. They looked overwhelmed and had assumed expressions proclaiming the burden of guilt by association. One poor fellow was trying to clean up the floors and looked like Mickey Mouse's Sorcerer's Apprentice, attempting to contain an out of control flood with a mop and bucket.

Another guest suddenly ran out from the bathroom. I remembered him as gentle and unassuming. He was now apparently under the influence of some sort of hallucinogenic and began pacing and ranting obscenities at invisible invaders. Our attempts to calm him failed. He ran back into the bathroom and then out again, this time his hand was bleeding from a self-inflicted cut. He passed out, his blood pouring onto the floorboards.

Leia and the sober guest quickly bandaged the fallen man's wound, carried him into the car and rushed him off to the emergency room. I was left behind with the repentant others who had by now become quite lucid. Someone brought me some rags and I found myself down on my knees, mopping up sour vomit and freshly spilled blood. And remarkably, there it was—that ever-elusive "now" place that I had hoped to find in a pristine little prayer room. That pivotal point wherein monastic enlightenment intersects with human misery and grace pours forth abundantly in the midst of splendid contradiction.

Thus, it was not in prayerful seclusion but in crowded pandemonium that I had my moment of truth. It was while on my hands and knees scrubbing the drippings of a poor man's sad stigmata off of floorboards with soapy water and bleach that I felt the first inkling of what it means to be engaged in both action and contemplation at one and the same moment. It was such an epiphanous realization that I grew hesitant while dipping my rag into a final repugnant puddle, afraid that I would disturb the reflection of the Face of God, for I was now sure that was exactly where God's Face was becoming manifest. Still on my knees, I reached into my pocket and touched the poem. Habits. They are messy. Seductive. Self-destructive. A nuisance. They dig into our souls. They bring us to our knees. They are the great levelers, leading us into the mystery of surrender. Hallelujah.

Tiffany: Mary's Word Resounding From the Maryland Hotel

A Reflection Interwoven with St. Bernard's Fourth Sermon on Mary, December 2014

> "Mary, you have been told that you shall conceive and bear a Son: you have heard that this shall be not by human means, but through the intervention of the Holy Spirit.

> Behold, the Angel now awaits your answer. We also, O Lady, await from your lips the sentence of mercy and compassion, we who are groaning under the sentence of our woundedness. For lo! The price of our salvation is now offered to you: if you will only consent, we shall at once be set at liberty. We have been created by the eternal Word of God, and behold we die: by your momentary word we much be renewed and restored to life."

Some years ago, while volunteering with the San Pedro Catholic Worker, I discovered that everyone who was poor in the area knew about the Maryland Hotel. Perhaps things are different now but back in those days the stairs were steep, the carpets, worn and stained, and the rooms, small. You had to fry your eggs in a common kitchen and walk down a long dreary hallway to use the communal bathroom. Cockroaches and mice were a nuisance but the rent was cheap and it beat sleeping on the sidewalks.

The upstairs room at the farthest end of the Maryland Hotel belonged to Tiffany and her three young nephews. The year that I befriended her, she made the difficult and painful decision to drop out of her classes at a local community college, where she was a straight 'A' student in Graphic Design, and become the full time caretaker of the three boys. Theirs was a crowded, stuffy living space yet Tiffany used her creativity to make the most of it. Since there was only one double bed in the tiny room, the kids slept in it while Tiffany slept on the floor with a pillow and blanket.

> "O Virgin! Most loving, Adam and Eve, now exiled from Paradise with all of their offspring, implore this favor of you. For this does Abraham entreat, for this David, for this all the other holy fathers and mothers, your own ancestors, who are now dwelling in the region of the shadow of death. See, the whole world, prostrate at your feet, awaits your answer. And not without cause. For on your word depend the consolation of the miserable, the redemption of the captives, the pardon of the condemned, the salvation of all the children of Adam and Eve, of the entire human rave. O Virgin, delay not to answer . . . "

The Mean Streets and the Desert

Tiffany's sister, Carrie,—the mother of the three little boys—was at that time serving out a jail sentence in Los Angeles. Her history read like a roller coaster ride. It seemed that most of her ups and downs involved drugs, rough men, unplanned pregnancies and a forgetfulness to pay cashiers on her way out of stores after shopping sprees. She was due to give birth while in custody to two more children—twins.

Each child in Carrie's life had a different father. Two were in prison, the other was homeless, uneducated and most of the time, broke. At the beginning of the school year, one father managed to sober up long enough to earn cash and buy his son a set of school clothes. The other boys went to school in patched up hand-me-downs.

Tiffany told me that she held no grudge against any of the fathers nor did she condemn her sister's promiscuity. Yet it was Tiffany, not the children's parents, who embraced responsibility for the little boys. She herself was fragile, yet she managed to sustain enough emotional strength and enough generosity of heart to hold it all together.

> "Make haste, therefore, to answer the Angel, or rather to answer the Lord through the Angel. Say the word and receive the Word. Utter your human word and conceive the divine Word. Pronounce the transitory word and embrace the Word everlasting. Why do you hesitate? Wherefore do you fear? Believe, consent, and receive into your womb the Word of the Father. Let your humility take courage, let your modesty be confident. It is in no wise expedient now that your virginal simplicity should be forgetful of prudence. O Virgin most prudent, in this matter alone you may put aside all fear of presumption, because although modesty pleases by its silence, yet more necessary for us now is the charity of your YES."

Tiffany, humbling herself, sometimes asked charity organizations for things like jackets and shoes for the boys. She never asked for clothes for herself although she confided in me that she felt embarrassed about her weight, and her large dress size. I responded that she radiated beauty through the softness of her face, the grace of her posture, the gentleness of her voice, her goodness, and had no cause for embarrassment.

The boys required her full attention. She walked the older ones to and from school, took them to the public library to do their homework, kept the youngest one close to her side and in the evenings they all went to the Catholic Worker soup line at the park for a hot meal. At the soup line, the boys always had groomed hair, smiling faces and clean hands. As long as Tiffany loved and consented to care for them, the boys knew that they would not have to be separated and placed in foster care.

> "O happy Virgin, open your heart to faith, open your lips to consent, open your bosom to your Creator. Behold the Desired of all nations is standing outside and knocking at your door. So tragic if He should pass on while you delay to open, and you should have to begin once more to seek with sorrow 'Him whom your soul loves'! Arise, therefore, and make haste to open to Him. Arise by faith, make haste by devotion, open by consent."

Relief from the poverty of the Maryland Hotel was not immediately at hand for Tiffany and the boys. The local agencies that raised funds to help families were restricted by regulations that did not include providing housing assistance to an aunt trying to keep her sister's children together as a family. Nonetheless, Tiffany persisted in seeking ways of moving them into decent housing.

Sometimes, when I would look for a moment into her eyes, I could perceive the gray fog of depression descending upon the landscape of her brave spirit, her weary soul. Yet when I would observe her for any length of time, I clearly saw her quiet yet persistent strength and her commitment to the future of these little ones who so needed her protection. One day, she declared to me that she was making efforts to bring the twins to the Maryland Hotel room after their birth. She was praying for a miracle because she didn't want the new babies to be adopted by strangers.

> "And Mary said, Behold the handmaiden of the Lord, be it done unto me according to your word."

The Mean Streets and the Desert

Unfortunately, I moved away from San Pedro to facilitate the High Desert Catholic Worker before anything was resolved about the twins or about the possibility of the family obtaining decent affordable housing. The day before I left, I made a final visit to the Maryland Hotel. I brought groceries, gave the boys some clothes and toys and gifted Tiffany with a new dress and shoes. Somewhat awkwardly, I attempted to explain to Tiffany that because of her 'YES' to love, nurture and provide for her sister's children, she was a true descendant of Mary. I did my best to convince her that an angel of God rustled protective wings over her each night as she lay down on the floor of her room and whispered into her ear while she slept: *"You are full of grace and the Lord is with you."*

Walter: A Baptism of Beans

The Salvation Army Homeless Project, February 1997

As the saying goes, I knew him back in the day. His street name was Pig Pen, not sure why, but I insisted on calling him by his given name, Walter. He was always in need of a roof over his head. When he wasn't in jail for repeated charges of public intoxication, he liked to sleep on-board the Banana Bus, a mobile homeless shelter, a hippie wagon on wheels operated by a fellow named Brad Goans and his volunteer crew.

It was a simple operation—each evening, a volunteer driver made rounds throughout the town, stopping at intervals to pick up homeless men. They could be inebriated but had to leave their bottles behind. Violent threats or actions were absolutely forbidden. When the Banana Bus was at full capacity, the driver would park it for the night on a vacant lot, courtesy of the sheriff, out on Kansas Avenue, just a stone's throw from the jail.

Twice a month I wrapped myself up in layers of warm clothes and volunteered along with a friend of mine to alternate keeping vigil outside the bus from dusk to dawn. While one of us slept on a cot, the other would sit in a folding chair, flashlight in hand, going inside the bus on the hour to check on the sleeping occupants.

Each Other's Angels

Some nights Walter stepped into the bus freshly washed with a grin on his face and other nights he stumbled in bleary eyed, stinking of cigarettes and alcohol. Whenever he was sober, he tended to the hobo fire–as he dubbed it–outside in the gravel pit. Sitting pensively on an old milk crate with a metal rod in his hand to guide wood into the flames, he appeared almost mystical beneath the stars and under the spell of firelight.

He wore a large crucifix on a cord around his neck and once declared himself a monastic of the streets. The cross, along with a hint of Boston in his voice, distinguished him from the other fellows who circled around the fire. One night after a day of imbibing, Walter started confessing the sins of his past to God with me as his witness.

His litany of trespasses and wrongful behaviors flowed from his mouth and fell to the ground like so many broken prayer beads. He wanted me to say something in Latin "To make it official" and all I could come up with on the spot was "Mea culpa . . . mea culpa . . . mea maxima culpa." He began striking his right fist fervently against his chest. After about five minutes of this, he announced abruptly that God had definitely forgiven him. So then, that was that. Walter had a clean slate. Off to bed he went, falling blissfully into a deep sleep.

Walter's eyes often gazed out into seeming nothingness. I sensed it was the look of a man longing to see through his own darkness, hoping for a shaft of light to break through, illuminate his shadowed spirit and banish phantoms that lurked in the gray corners of his soul. At other times, those same eyes could sparkle unexpectedly in a mirthful and mischievous manner that one might expect from a Lost Boy in Never Land

One evening, Walter began discoursing philosophically—in a style that only he could pull off—about problems that arise in towns like our own when people perceive two populations: *them* and *us*. "So now, you see Toni, I am a one of *them*, homeless, penniless and usually drunk as a skunk. I provide a necessary service for the persons who see me as despicable because I reinforce their secure sense of being a one of *us*, the *us* being people who have

The Mean Streets and the Desert

jobs and families and homes. And Toni, I hate to tell you this, but you seem to be hovering back and forth between both the *them* folks here on Kansas Avenue and the *us* folks who live everywhere else. What gives?"

We both paused and I trembled over his question. Or maybe it was just a chill in the air that caught me. We sat together for another hour or so—he with his question and me with no answer—under the same indifferent night sky hearing the same indiscriminate log crackle in the open fire.

The Banana Bus is now long gone and Walter, who moved into a sober house after qualifying for disability payments, died last year. He was only 54 years old. I didn't learn the cause of his death. Bless his soul. I'm left behind, yet to fully resolve the trembling question. Where is my strongest alliance—with marginal folks like the guys on Kansas Avenue or with people who maintain a solid social standing in the community? Indeed, what gives? Must I choose? I want a connection with both!

I have a grand memory though, of feeling completely at home, hanging out by the open fire one cold midnight with Walter, a couple of his buddies and a can of beans. I grabbed that can of beans, and using a length of coat hanger, suspended it unopened, directly over the flames. Walter cautioned, "Whoa there. That's not the way you cook beans." But I was sure I knew what I was doing and wanted to show them all that I was no longer a campsite greenhorn.

And oh the holy rolling beans as they exploded from the can . . . the squishy, soft rolling, beans and the stars and the beans and the golden redeeming sparks from the fire . . . yes, the sparks from the fire and Walter and the guys all laughing with beans in their hair . . . the redeeming beans . . . the beans slapping and sloshing and painting my face . . . and oh those beans . . . all over my shoes and my jeans . . . beans splattering on my jacket and my heart and my soul . . . we all marveled as beans rained down on the tops of our heads . . . and for a suspended moment we were, all of us together, one with the beans . . . what a Baptism!

Chapter 2

Protests and Jails

But all I can say—on the wing—is: it's possible. Come on!

—Daniel Berrigan, *The Bird*

Alice: Angel Under The Broom Tree

Crisp County Jail, August, 2002

Elijah went into the wilderness and came and sat down under a solitary broom tree. He asked that he might die. "It is enough; now O Lord, take away my life, for I am no better than my ancestors." Then he lay down under the broom tree and fell asleep. Suddenly, an angel touched him and said to him "Get up and eat."

—1 Kings

Protests and Jails

The message from my friend and support person, Alice, who lives in Columbus, Georgia, came to me over the telephone and shattered my spirits. "Brace yourself," she warned, as she informed me that the Regional Bureau of Prisons had resolved not to transport me, as originally planned, to the relative comfort of the women's Federal Minimal Security Camp in Dublin, California where lots of sunshine, outdoor space and decent food awaited me as well as the opportunity to enjoy long visits from nearby family members and friends. Instead, I must remain in custody here in the Crisp County Jail in Cordele, Georgia—for the duration of my sentence. Alice guessed I would soon be segregated from the regular female jail population in a lockdown cell to avoid possible controversy and conflict since there had been publicity about my being here as a prisoner of conscience.

I'd already endured several days in the bleakness of the Muscogee County jail and then a week at the Harris County jail and was expecting to be here in the Crisp County jail for no more than two weeks. The two weeks were up. It was more than I could psychologically bear—the devastating news that I would not be flown home to California. I would not complete my time at a detention camp with an athletic track and green belts and trees. I would not be able to see my family.

If indications of being in shock include feeling simultaneously cold and sweaty, nauseated and unfocused, weak and unable to take a full breath, then I was in a sorry state of shock. I curled up in my bunk and stayed there for hours without eating or even lifting my head off the mattress. A few of my fellow inmates, who had grown accustomed to my routine of sitting on my bunk with a novel in my hand, praying before my meals, writing at the day room table, playing card games, and diligently attending to my hygiene, asked me about my sudden reclusive behavior. I didn't care to answer so I said nothing. I wanted to sleep and forget my fate.

The next day, Alice showed up as my visitor. I really didn't want to visit with anyone, not even Alice. Rather, I felt embarrassed at the prospect of her seeing me in my sorry state. I was no longer the brave peace protester she had last seen, I had morphed into a broken spirited inmate. Dark half-moon circles had formed under my eyes. My hair was unkempt, my skin lackluster and pale. But then I gave thought of her kindness, knowing she had driven two and a half hours just to spend forty-five minutes with me, I allowed myself to be escorted to the visiting area.

On the way to the visiting center, I reflected on how Alice appears in every way to be a perfectly human woman and how I'm convinced she is really an angel. For years, she and her husband have been active community members in Columbus and she has volunteered her time supporting the efforts of Roy Bougeois—her neighbor and a champion of human rights—to shut down the notorious School of the Americas at Fort Benning. Most significantly, Alice has generously dedicated herself to sustaining the spirits of non-violent U.S. prisoners of conscience by ordering books for us and writing letters to us and visiting those of us who are incarcerated in Georgia. That's the stuff of angels.

Within seconds of seeing Alice through the glass partition, I felt more focused and my heart quickened with a hint of joy just to see a smile on her forthright face. We spoke into phones on each side of the glass and Alice's words were full of promise and encouragement. Toward the end of our allotted time, Alice said, "Even though it's unlikely that you'll get transferred, people on the outside are advocating for you. Don't lose hope!" And I saw her give a correctional officer a Catholic bible with my name on it, complete with a scripture list that coordinates with the Liturgical Calendar. And, perhaps for purposes of extending ironic humor my way, she threw in a paperback of Dostoevsky's *Crime and Punishment*. I admit to grinning.

Upon returning to my cell, it didn't take me long to fall into my former funk. What if all the advocacy in the world doesn't work in my favor and I'm forced to remain at Crisp County Jail through January of 2003? I plopped myself onto my bunk and drifted into an abstraction of vague, disturbing dreams. I awoke later to the screams of another woman who had just been brought to D-3. When new inmates arrive they are often hung-over or still high, distraught, irritable, unhappy, sore-ridden, bruised, ashamed or filled with rage. This woman was afflicted with all of these maladies rolled together. She ranted, raved and shouted out a string of ghastly profanities. After about an hour, she finally reduced her outburst to a tearful whimper, took the bunk across from mine and slipped into an exhausted sleep,

I was relieved that she fell asleep. Ruckuses do break out between new comers and the women who have been incarcerated for a period of time. It might begin with *Shut up!* And move quickly into bouts of pushing, shoving, slapping and hair pulling. At first such incidents terrified and appalled me. I soon enough realized that it's sadly a part of jail life. There's seems to be no other ready outlet for frustration. The jail staff, for the most part, remains curt, remote, seemingly indifferent, and of course they hold the keys; the judges, lawyers, juries are all in the distant past; the society that deems addiction a crime and not an illness is unreachable and has already won its hand against them. And so, I've concluded that my fellow inmates turn on each other when confinement and overcrowding bear down upon them and their frustrations get the best of them.

As for my own circumstances, it dawned on me after visiting with Alice that I was most likely stuck here for the next five months and had three choices . . . to succumb to depression and self pity, to begin throwing tantrums that would further upset an already unsettled cell block, or to rise up and extend compassion to my fellow inmates. It was a no brainer to choose the third option. I pulled myself from bed, took a shower and combed my hair. When dinner arrived, I gently awakened the new woman and offered her a seat next to mine at the meal table. Sitting down, she said, "I'm Sharonda." I replied, "I'm Toni." A beginning. The kitchen had not yet received her name so she had no food tray. I gave her my salad and my bread. Alice had been my angel—now it was my turn. "Eat," I urged, "it will help."

He looked, and there at his head was a cake baked on hot stones and a jar of water. He ate and drank and lay down again. The angel of the Lord came a second time, touched him, and said, "Get up and eat again, otherwise the journey will be too much for you." He got up and ate and drank . . .

—1 Kings

Dora Jean Raises the Cross in Jail

San Luis Obispo, California, 2013

One morning a few years ago, after a prolonged season of loss and grief, I came face to face with myself in my bathroom mirror and recognized a twice divorced, sixty-something year old grandmother in need of a full time job. Having spent years volunteering as a Catholic Worker and decades working for non-profit agencies serving the needs of poor people on the fringes of society, I decided to seek less intense employment—something that would allow me some semblance of serenity. I prayed for God to lead me to a quiet monastery that had a Help Wanted sign posted in the front window.

Often, God has plans for us other than the ones we seek. And while I was applying for jobs in quiet settings, an opportunity was presented to me for work at the local county jail, preparing destitute women with psychiatric and addiction challenges for release, and for some crazy reason, I said yes. It was a surprise to be approved for employment at the jail, having myself already served jail time for a misdemeanor in the state of Georgia, a result of participating in a non-violent act of civil disobedience, namely trespassing onto a military base. However, the interview panel seemed to think of that as an experiential advantage for the women inmates.

At first, I worried a lot about what I could offer the women. Their lives were already stained and darkened with histories of madness, cravings and abuse. Billy, an enigmatic character in the film *The Year of Living Dangerously*, says at one point, "I support the view that you just do whatever you can about the misery that's in front of you. Add your light to the sum of light." With that in mind, I began to show up each morning at the women's jail, push the button that opens the metal entry door and try my best to shed a bit of light into the shadowed existence of each woman I encountered.

Correctional officers would deliver kites—jail talk for request slips—to my office from inmates who wanted to see me for guidance, needs assessments, referrals and discharge plans. Once they were escorted to the waiting area, I would call them in, one by one, and we would sit together while I listened to their respective stories. Although some were held in custody awaiting trial dates for serious and violent charges, most were serving time for trespassing, illegal drug offenses, drunk and disorderly behavior, prostitution, writing bad checks or shoplifting.

One memorable young woman, Dora Jean, who was convicted on multiple non-violent drug charges, spent almost a year in custody and began seeing me on a regular basis, two or three times a week. She was skinny, pale and toothless with a plethora of tattoos that failed to fully cover the needle marks and scabs that ran up and down her arms and legs like miniature train tracks. She never asked to see the psychiatrist for medication or for my assistance in making release plans, or for anything, really other than for me to listen while she breathed, cried and guided herself through a variety of emotions, everything from grief to anger to the edge of despair to the brink of unfamiliar hope. And in that way, she unwittingly commissioned me to the task of doing whatever I could for the misery in front of me, and invited me to add my light to the sum of light.

Visit after visit, over months of time, this young woman sat before me and I learned that the best way to lighten her burden was to let her 'be'—be sad, be scared, be remorseful, be angry, be resentful, be resigned, be strong, be hopeful, be at peace. And when she eventually stopped requesting to see me, I heard from a custody officer that she had begun attending a bible group. I wished she would have decided to go to bible study *and* still have visits with me, but then I asked myself, who am I to begrudge someone for wanting to study the bible as an exclusive focus? The important thing was for this woman to receive more light, from whatever source she chose.

The day before she was due for release, a custody officer brought Dora Jean to see me at her request. She thanked me for the time I had spent with her and in turn, I smiled and reminded her that she was leaving the jail with a clean new page of life. After exchanging these farewells, she pulled out a wrinkled piece of paper from her jumper pocket and handed it to me saying, "This is a message from The Jesus People. It's all I have to give you." I accepted it, not having a clue as to what was or who were The Jesus People. When alone in my office, I read the flyer and realized that the young woman was raising the Cross on her way out of jail and encouraging me to continue to do the same by tending the women still behind bars.

> "We simply argue that the Cross be raised again in the jailhouse and at the center of the market place as well as on the steeple of the church. Jesus was not crucified in a cathedral between two candles, but on a Cross between two thieves; on a town garbage heap; at a crossroad so cosmopolitan that His title was written in Hebrew, Latin, and Greek; at the kind of place where cynics talk smut and thieves curse and soldiers gamble. That is where He died and that is what He died about, and that is where church folk need to be and what church folk need to be about."

"Amen!" I shouted this from behind my office desk to no one in particular and to everyone.

Jerry, Phil and Dan

Crisp Co, Jail, December 7, 2002

It's almost unheard of in county jails and prisons to place men and women in cells that are next to each other. Most often, there is a building designated for men and a separate one designated for women. Smaller jail facilities, with only one building, usually place the male population in units that are at the opposite end of a long corridor from the female population, sealed off by heavy metal electronic doors.

However, in this jail, my friend Jerry, surprisingly and serendipitously is my next-door neighbor. Jerry Zawada—Franciscan priest, fellow SOA prisoner of conscience, radical peacemaker, champion of the poor and oppressed, war resister, and to use a traditional term, a gentleman possessing both kindness and inner strength. And he loves to laugh. I like to tell him that he's a saint with a sense of humor. Whenever I say this, he dismisses the saint part and confirms the humor part by telling a couple of ridiculously corny jokes, laughing at them himself.

Jerry declares our being placed in cells that share a common wall a miracle. Most likely our placement was due to the fact that we were Federal prisoners. Upon transferring here from the Harris County jail, we spent our first two weeks respectively confined with the regular male and female jail population. Then the sheriff made a decision to segregate us from the local inmates and he reassigned us to the only two lock-down cells in the jail, meaning we were confined to our cells for an average of twenty-three out of every twenty-four hours.

The common wall between our cells has two sets of air vents, one installed near the floor base and the other placed up near the ceiling above the toilets. These vents have become our favorite (and only!) devices for communicating with each other. Although sometimes we bend down and chat through the lower vent, Jerry and I agree that we prefer the challenge of standing on our toilets (not an easy feat!) to converse and pray together. We joke about how proficiently we engage in "toilet talk"! And we both admit to feeling subversively delighted in discovering such an ingenious way to visit.

Thanks to the vents, we often read letters from friends and supporters to each other; regularly recite morning and evening prayer together; share the importance of remaining strong in spirit and in solidarity with the innocent victims who suffered, died or disappeared at the hands of the SOA graduates. This, we remind ourselves, is why we are here. Honestly, I don't know if I could get through even one more day of incarceration but for Jerry's availability. I thank God every day for his presence next door.

Both of our cells are two person cells with two bunks. I have only one 'cellie' and so I have my own bunk, toilet, and sink—quite a luxury! However, when the jail staff learned that Jerry was a Catholic priest who spoke fluent Spanish, they began placing three to four Spanish-speaking men at a time in with Jerry. And of course, Jerry, in his true Franciscan way, always forfeits the bunks over to his cellmates, sharing the floor with the remaining men. The men housed with Jerry seem to derive solace and spiritual consolation from his presence and the fact that he speaks their language must surely be a comfort. They look to him as their confessor, life coach, friend, and parent figure. And they eat well because periodically, Jerry restricts his diet to water and juice, fasting for peace, and giving his food to his cellmates.

Today, December 7th, just after breakfast, I hear Jerry calling to me through the upper air-vent and his usually jovial voice is somber. I go over and stand on the toilet, put my ear to the vent, and listen to his sad disclosure. *Toni. He's dead.* I pause and then ask who is dead and he responds that while listening to National Public Radio on his transistor, a newscaster interrupted regular programming. He announced that Philip Berrigan, long time non-violent Catholic peace activist, died at home on December 6th of cancer at age 79, leaving behind his brothers, Daniel, John, Jim and Jerry as well as his wife, Elizabeth McAlister, their three children and many fellow peacemakers.

I know how sad Jerry must feel since he and Phil were personal friends, pioneers of peaceful protesting in the U.S., opposing war and violence throughout decades of time. I never had the privilege of meeting Phil in person but he has written letters of inspiration and support to both Jerry and me, even though he was himself weak and ill. I have, however, met Daniel Berrigan on several occasions. In fact, I've had an innocent crush on him for decades, feeling much like Judy Garland must have felt when

Protests and Jails

singing to Clark Gable's photo in a 1938 movie, "Dear Mr. Gable, you made me love you . . . "

Daniel, in his capacity as a Jesuit priest, was once facilitating a retreat I attended in Santa Barbara, California. and we took a stroll together during a lunch break. After confiding in me that his favorite film star had been Jean Harlow—quite a disclosure in and of itself—I learned first hand from him how he and Phil made history when in 1968, they burned Vietnam War draft files in Catonsville, Maryland. They met with harsh consequences. Dan went on to tell me how later, as a married family man, Phil continued to live his life as a civil rights and antiwar activist. Over the years, both brothers spent time in various prisons for acts of civil disobedience. Both were leaders in the Plowshares movement—a highly controversial campaign of civil disobedience against arms trade and nuclear weapons. Yet they also prayed regularly and devotedly and encouraged others in the peace movement to do the same.

At the time of this writing, Daniel, who is in his 80's, must be deeply grieving the loss of his brother, yet I know he will remain an inspiring presence in the Peace Movement. When God one day takes Daniel to join Philip in Paradise, the many books he has authored and his volumes of poetry will be his tangible legacy for the world. And it's my opinion that Dan's decision to visit hospitals and hospices—away from public view—ministering to wounded war veterans, and those suffering from cancer and AIDS, will be the entrance ticket he hands to the Angel at the Gate.

As for Philip, at this moment, neither Jerry nor I would be shocked, frightened or unsettled if he were to drop in here right now for a visit with us—like Christ did with the Apostles in the Upper Room—as he transitions from earthly life into a fuller more radiant life with God. He would be right at home here, having been accustomed to doing time behind bars, having sacrificed years of his life inside of prisons and jails in prophetic witness. We certainly feel his presence on a spiritual level.

Jerry and I begin to pray the Rosary for the repose of Phil Berrigan's soul and for members of his surviving family. We murmur back and forth to each other the Our Fathers and Hail Mary's of the Glorious Mysteries, and we can almost hear Phil's voice resonating with our own, as the prayers drift through the air ducts into every corner of the jail and far beyond the locked doors.

Kaya and Tammy: Lessons in Lockdown

Crisp County Jail, December 2002

For the last five months of my six-month prison sentence, I was in lockdown inside a two-person cell at the Crisp County Jail. Kaya, an attractive, slender young Black woman in her twenties, was my cellmate for four months. Lockdown meant that we remained in our cell for 23 out of 24 hours each day. In truth, we were often locked in for entire 72-hour periods. The cell was a self contained set-up having three sections, a day room—with a metal table and two metal chairs, a shower, a toilet, a T.V., a phone, a food slot and a metal door, both opening into the hallway when unlocked—and two sleeping cubicles, each with a sealed 10" by 4" window, small desk, footlocker, lower bunk, toilet and sink. Everything moveable was bolted to the cement floor.

We were segregated from the regular population for different reasons: I was not in county custody, rather a Federal prisoner being housed in a county jail. And my arrest at the SOA non-violent protest, even though a misdemeanor, had been publicized in local newspapers. Kaya, from what little I could gather, had been living with her small children at some sort of religious commune that was under some sort of investigation, Apparently, there were multiple arrests and Kaya did disclose that the leader of the commune was convicted of the most serious charges and ended up in prison. I never probed Kaya further about her legal situation and she never volunteered much more information. In time I did learn that she had MS—another probable reason for her being separated from the general population.

While the regular population had daily outings to the yard—and therefore to fresh air and sunlight, passes to go to the library and jobs (such as laundry duty), we only mingled with other inmates when we received permission to go to bible study and Sunday services. We were marched alone to and from our occasional trips to the yard, the medical clinic and the visiting area.

Eventually, I learned that Kaya was originally from New York, where her father worked as a fireman. Her mother, she said, was schizophrenic. She had never been to Georgia or any other part of the South until she became involved with the leader of the commune. She confided that she missed her children and her father and felt sad at having been deprived of a stable mother's nurturing. It was only natural that over time I became a sort of mother figure to her and she filled the hole in my heart, being so far from my own children and grandchildren.

And besides, I really liked Kaya. She prayed before every meal and read her bible throughout the day and evening. Each week, when friends brought her three little children to visit, she would braid her hair, wash her face and smooth out her orange jumper so that they could see that she was well and in good spirits.

Mornings in our cell, Kaya and I would exercise to Denise Austin's Pilates show, using unopened water bottles as weights. We found additional ways to transcend the tension and tedium of doing time, reading books out loud to each other or making up stories or telling corny jokes. And we often had mother–daughter type chats about fashion, family, and other feminine topics.

Three times a day, we sat and ate our food together. Often we complained at how every food item appeared to be either beige (think hard biscuits, cold grits, stale toast, lumpy mashed potatoes) or brown (as in watery coffee, tepid gravy, and what we called "mystery meat", a sort of processed ground and breaded meat and cereal blend). In compensation, I would pull out the Food Section of the L.A. Sunday Times that my CW friend, Jeff, regularly mailed to me under the guise of "spiritual material", and we would place colorful photos of mouth–watering meals such as pot roast with onions and carrots, peaches and cream tarts, spinach quiche and baked coconut shrimp with curried apricot sauce on our table and pretend that we were eating out in a fancy restaurant.

Each Other's Angels

I cried when Kaya was released in November although I was overjoyed knowing that she would be reunited with her children and would have opportunities to begin a new and better chapter in her life. My sadness over losing her as my constant companion was interrupted soon enough on a pre-dawn morning in early December when a custody officer escorted a frantic and fevered inmate into the cell and placed her on what had been Kaya's bunk. Another custody officer brought in a bucket of ice and some thin white washcloths. After they both left, locking the door behind them, I bent over my new 'cellie', Tammy, pale, blond, blue-eyed and freckle-faced and obviously in a state of misery. Her face was flushed, her eyes bright with fever, and she was cursing like a drunken sailor.

After about an hour, Tammy seemed to have slipped into a delirious state, tossing and turning and swearing nonsensically. I guessed that she was in serious withdrawal from alcohol or who knows what drugs or had a serious infection or the flu. I pushed the intercom system and yelled "This woman needs medical assistance right away!" The curt reply was "That's why we put her in lockdown and brought in the ice. Cover her up and keep her head cool. She'll be OK by tomorrow."

And that was that. I dipped a cloth into the ice water, wrung it out, folded it and placed it on Tammy's burning hot forehead. For at least three hours I knelt at Tammy's bunk, applying cold cloths on her face and under her neck and feeding her chips of ice at intervals. She wove in and out of sleep and finally she began to sweat profusely. Her fever had broken. It was only then that I realized how powerless I would have been if she would have had a seizure or fallen off the bunk or stopped breathing. It also passed through my mind, rather selfishly, that if she had anything contagious I could become sick myself.

The next morning, Tammy asked me my name and thanked me for helping her out. However, as days with her turned into weeks, I discovered that Tammy was a torment as a cellmate. She jumped about like a nervous colt, hogged the shower, stole snack food and other items from my personal supplies and retained her fondness for spewing four letter words at the top of her lungs. She soon developed a new habit of making excessively seductive phone calls to her boyfriend. And lacking other drugs of choice, she swallowed as many aspirins as the med person would dish out. She drove me crazy!

I have only a couple of weeks left in custody and Tammy remains my cellmate. The paradoxical thing is that I'm growing fond of her. She pasted photos of her kids—long ago removed from her care—on the wall and kisses them good night. I admire her audacity, spunk and stubborn pride and her survivability. Just as I had felt a kinship with Kaya because she was so loveable, I feel drawn to Tammy because she is so difficult.

None of us chose to be thrown together. The fates, however, determined that for a period of time, we share this small, gloomy, locked space doing jail time in Georgia. Kaya has already returned to New York. Before long, I'll be home in California. Tammy will soon thereafter be back on the streets here in Cordele, Georgia. And yet...

We are all in the same boat in a stormy sea and we owe each other a terrible loyalty.

—G.K. Chesterton

Kimberly in Ordinary Time

Crisp County Jail, 2002

Her name was Kimberly. Since she wasn't Catholic, she probably wouldn't have known that she lived out her last days in Ordinary Time—the weeks on the Liturgical Calendar that unfold in between the greater Church seasons of Lent/Easter and Advent/Christmas.

Regrettably, in jails and prisons, humans must count the misery of their days without respect to sacred cycles. Prisoners measure their stay as hard time or program time or short time—all suffer, some get sick, a few die and are buried and forgotten. No big deal. Nothing special. Except that it's the Body of Christ, perpetually broken.

According to the ladies who taught us bible lessons at the jail, Kimberly was a well-known 'revolving door' inmate, repeatedly serving short periods of incarceration for minor addiction related offenses. Apparently, Kimberly was in and out of here two or three times during the months I was in lockdown with my cellmate, Kathy, and neither of us had an opportunity to meet her because our bible study classes were on different days.

I might never have even heard about her or the fact that her death occurred just yards away from me but for the news of her passing on a local TV newscast. The report noted that a young woman had been booked into the Crisp County Jail, complaining of feeling ill and a couple of days later, she was found dead in her solitary cell.

During bible study the following week, everyone was talking about Kimberly's death. A couple of women disclosed to us and the church ladies that soon after her she had been brought into custody, Kimberly had been segregated from the general female jail population after she continued to complain of feeling sick. According to the covert communication network that runs between inmate custodians and the rest of the population, she was then confined in a padded isolation cell where later, she died, alone and apparently untended. Rumor had it that after her body was discovered, she was quickly removed from the premises without ceremony. Our bible study class joined the church ladies in saying prayers for Kimberly's soul. That's about all any of us could do on her behalf.

For a long time after that, I wished I didn't know about Kimberly's tragic fate. I wished I didn't know about the poor conditions of this and other jails in Georgia; the inadequate care, and the thousand and one indignities endured day-in and day-out by the inmates. But of course, I *do* know because I myself am an ordinary inmate doing ordinary time under anything but ordinary circumstances.

The irony is that throughout much of my adult life I strived to be extraordinary—to find my way into unique and heroic situations, fulfilling a teenage dream of helping to save the world. Last November, when I knelt down with fellow peace activists on military property to pray and protest the atrocities taught at the School of the Americas, I risked arrest and incarceration with the good intention of wanting to be a witness for justice. My heart was sincere yet I was also caught up in the surrealistic thrill of it all. According to Gandhi, "The truth seeker should go to jail even as a bridegroom enters the bridal chamber." That's the romantic experience I expected—that my jail time would be a noble act of love and sacrifice for the larger good and that I would remain strong in spirit.

Now, however, my passion, pride and idealism have dissipated into the mundane realities that every inmate faces—locked doors, tedium, monotony, cold food, thin blankets, fear, frustration, powerlessness, humiliation, degradation. Phil Berrigan once wrote, "No one of us likes jail. Yet we transcend this pit of misery, we shrug, grin, and bear it. In measure, we help humanize it." I now acutely grasp the meaning of his concrete message. I take hope in his words.

I was interviewed yesterday. A representative of the Regional Bureau of Prisons asked me about jail conditions and I told her many true things including my concern about Kimberly's untimely death. Maybe my testimony will prompt positive changes in here and maybe not. These outcomes are far beyond my reach. What *are* within my reach are the women in my bible study class and my cellmate, Kaya, with whom I share grits and eggs, disappointment and hope, and Ordinary Time. Six months to be exact.

Miss Wanda

Muscogee Co. Jail, Columbus, Georgia, July 19, 2002

It's day number 7 of my 182 day prison sentence and I've yet to receive my own pen, paper, stamps or envelopes. The pencil and paper I'm using right now is a borrowed one, kindness of a fellow inmate who also loaned me some stamps and envelopes.

My eyeglasses and my watch are the only personal items I was allowed to keep after I was booked into custody, and I'm immensely grateful for both. Upon entering the locked unit, I was issued a frayed plastic mattress, about two inches thick, which I have since laid out on the catwalk (a narrow platform on the second tier of the cellblock between the outside railing and the cells). This is because I have no sleeping cell. I also have no toilet of my own and must bribe others with candy bars (purchased from the jail commissary guard on my first day) in order to use the toilets in their cells.

I'm not the only one sleeping on the catwalk. There are twenty-two cells, each with a double bunk and a toilet, and there are over ninety women currently occupying the cellblock. The loudest and boldest women claim the bunks and toilets, leaving the concrete floor and the catwalk for the rest of us to place our mattresses upon.

The main level common room is large and looks like the inside hollow of an ancient tree trunk. It's dank, cold and windowless except for the shatter proof, double paned glass that looks out onto the corridor and the guards' station. In addition to several steel tables and benches that are bolted to the concrete floor, the common room is furnished with living bodies or as one guard rudely termed it, 'flooded with inmate overflow'. Some clever women put their mattresses on top of the tables at night. It's a way to avoid being stepped on in your sleep.

On my second day, I was given a plastic cup, a toothbrush, a comb, a bar of soap, a roll of toilet paper, a towel, and a thin, smelly blanket. By day number three, my plastic cup and comb had been spirited away while I slept. On day number four, I spotted my towel wrapped around the shampooed head of one of my 'celli's'.

Protests and Jails

It looked like she had my soap in her hand as well. By the time I received replacements, I had deduced that it's best to sleep with my cup, toothbrush, comb, soap, toilet paper and towel hidden under my blanket.

Today it's slowly dawning on me that I'm really locked away from the outside world. Far away from loved ones. From stores and houses and parks. From the sun, wind, moon and stars. From trees and flowers and birds and big wide blue skies. A woman who has been locked inside here for six months waiting for a court date, revealed that she never has visitors and is yet to see the light of day or feel the outdoor air even though there is a jail stipulation that the courtyard be made available to inmates for daily exercise.

The worst part of this scenario is the noise level. A television is mounted on the wall while a transistor radio remains on a shelf opposite the T.V. in such a way that sounds from both compete back and forth across the room at ear-splitting levels from pre-dawn until well after midnight. Even that clamor is overpowered by inmates' deafening screams, shrieks, wails and howls, which ceaselessly echo throughout the cellblock. There is no way to escape the horridly distorted T.V. and radio noise nor the riotous, exquisitely painful cries of addicts detoxing from street drugs, alcoholics in the midst of delirium tremors and mentally ill souls lost in the tangled and invisible taunts of phantom voices. I've tried putting toilet paper in my ears but it doesn't really alleviate the noise.

In a desperate attempt to seek some sort of compensatory comfort, I requested—and was subsequently denied—permission to see a Catholic priest or a Eucharistic minister. I am without a rosary, Communion services, or any way to follow the liturgical readings of the day. This is Bible Belt country, yet I'm incarcerated without a Bible.

Surprises happen, though, even in this sorry southern jail. Yesterday, into the deprivation of my surroundings, burst a light—Miss Wanda, a white Baptist preacher lady, visibly afflicted with some sort of palsy and thus wheelchair-bound. With some effort, she rolled herself through the locked steel entrance door and into our day room whereupon she immediately began giving 'witness' to a few women, obviously familiar to her, who huddled around her motorized chair.

I'm at a loss to tell you how her presence graced and revived the atmosphere in the room! Her words, as she preached, were deceptively simple. I perceived her as someone very close to God because she emanated such loving acceptance toward all the inmates, myself included. Miss Wanda re-told the Old Testament story of Joseph in the pit and looked right at me while she spoke. I suppose I stood out a bit since I was obviously not Black, not street wise, and not jail smart! "Are you one of those SOA protesters I read about in the papers, honey?" I nodded a hesitant "yes" to which Miss Wanda replied with elongated eloquence, "Honey-darlin', you are privileged like Joseph who was betrayed by his brothers. You are here in this pit of forsakenness as a testament to your faith and don't lose sight of that, honey."

To another—a Black woman whose dark eyes twitched in their sockets uncontrollably and whose facial skin wept with open sores—she said, "You and I are alike, you see? You are locked in this jail and I am locked in this chair. Still and all, we are both free to accept the love of Jesus." The woman's wild eyes kept on twitching and her sores persisted in oozing but she was able to execute a responsive smile.

Encouraged, Miss Wanda began to sway in her chair, turning its wheels with her hands, first toward one woman and then toward another and yet another, asking, "Now tell me, do y'all want to be Saved?" There wasn't a person in the room who didn't cry, "Yes, umm hmm, yes." So, when my time arrived, what else could I do? Miss Wanda asked me, did I want to be Saved, and I said, "Yes I do Miss Wanda." And so it happened that—deprived of Catholic consolations—Jesus saved me anyway, courtesy of a Baptist deliverer in an electric wheelchair named Miss Wanda.

After Miss Wanda left us, the positive energy she had introduced into the cellblock seemed to dissipate and was replaced all too quickly with the heaviness of despondency. There are so many layers of poverty in this horrid place. We are entombed in the filth of a neglected jail in the bowels of Georgia. The drab walls of the cellblock are chipping and peeling and hope is fading fast in this facility, exposing old cinder block and fresh despair.

Every day at 4:00 AM, I'm awakened from restless sleep patterns into the utter absurdity of 'head count' by stern security guards. At 5:00 AM, I'm given a tray of cold grits, muddy coffee, and a slice of white, untoasted, butterless bread. Afterwards, I wait in line with 90 others for a chance to rinse myself in one of the two working showers. Even if I miraculously find one of the phones free, I hardly ever make a call. It's impossible to hear anything above the endemic babble and blare of the environment.

I sense the collective brooding bubbling in the pressure cooker of this milieu; the violence that lies dormant within the inmates. Anything, from spilled salt to a fight on the "Jerry Springer Show," can trigger aggression and set someone off on someone else. A couple of days ago, one woman attacked another woman and gashed her skull open, banging her body against one of the metal tables and throwing her, head first, down onto the concrete floor . . . all because of a half-eaten chocolate bar that they both claimed as "mine."

This is the obscure and twisted micro—world of socially unacceptable and seemingly forgotten souls, Black women and a few white women like myself, integrated into the mutual poverty of the Muscogee County jail—prostitutes, strippers, drug addicts, embezzlers, check forgers, drunks and one lone SOA protester. Thank God for Miss Wanda, who breaks through the misery and reminds us that we are, now and forever, God's beloved children—remembered and therefore redeemed.

Officer C.

Muscogee Co. Jail, July 2002

For the life of me, I can't remember her actual name. The inmates called her Officer C. She was tall, attractive, with coal black hair, ebony eyes, and a complexion like chocolate silk. Her metal-toed boots were always spit-shined, her olive green uniform was consistently starched and impeccably creased. She might have been somebody's wife, mother to a couple of kids, the choir leader at the church on the corner. I'll never know the personal details of her life. I only know, that for the first two weeks of my incarceration after trespassing onto military property in protest against the School of the Americas, she served as my captor at the old Muscogee County Women's Jail wherein I began my season of captivity.

She was the guard who escorted me from the processing room, down the corridor, into the women's jail, and through two sets of electronically operated solid steel doors that opened and swallowed me—like the jaws of a motorized beast—into cell block 119. In fact, Officer C. practically pushed me into the day room and then abruptly turned her straight shouldered back on my crestfallen face, marching off to fulfill her duties elsewhere. What runs through her veins, I asked myself silently and sarcastically, ice water?

The cell-block threatened all my sensibilities. Imagine if you will, visions of a dungeon in the Dark Ages or a film clip from the classic 1948 movie, The Snake Pit. The place was a dark hole—dirty, dank, foul-smelling, and dismal. I stood aghast before this arena of oppression, built decades ago to hold something like 40 inmates but now housing over 90 women. Some were crammed like sardines inside of narrow sleeping cells while others dangled legs and arms over the railings constructed along the upper tier, and still more lay curled under thin blankets on floor mats in the day room. It dawned on me that caged animals in city zoos were allotted more space than these women. And now I was included amongst them.

Because of the high ceilings, hard cement floor, and bare stone walls, the sound blasting from the television set mingled with the shrill screams of detoxing crack addicts and the babble of hallucinating bag ladies, producing excruciating measures of noise. After an hour of uninterrupted exposure to these excessively heightened decibels of sound, I was beside myself, narcissistically surmising that this was some sort of conspiracy—a form of torture implemented by the veteran inmates upon me, the newcomer. At first, I wished I were deaf and then later I feared I soon would be if no one intervened or the TV didn't self-destruct.

Someone did intervene. Officer C. reentered the day room and turned off the television. Her jaw was set in such a way that you knew if you challenged her you would surely become mince meat pie on her dinner plate. You could have heard a pin drop. She began to pace the hushed room, slowly and deliberately, like a panther on the prowl for prey. It was with grim certainty that I prepared myself for a lecture to rival Revelation's pronouncements of Judgment Day. But I was wrong. "That's better," was all she said to the now mute crowd of women. Then, as before, she turned her back and exited through both sets of automatic doors—the doors that separated "petty criminals" from "correctional authorities."

The next few days left me no doubt that I was a part of the "petty criminal" group, so grim and powerless a creature did I become in my own eyes. I slept—or didn't—under the invisible insignia of fear. I fought the instinct to gag on my meager and cold meals. I cringed each time the boldest of the women squabbled amongst themselves, threatening to throw chairs and tossing up obscenities like so much confetti.

I soon figured out that aggression served as a way to fend off despair, and that with a distorted sense of bravado, the strongest women often opted to fight rather than surrender to hopelessness. The corner cells were called "Heartbreak Hotels." In each one, you could catch a glimpse of half-hidden forms—those broken women who had given up the fight, their vacant eyes explaining the conditions of their souls and sad histories gutted by poverty, mental illness, and the effects of street drugs.

What would become of me in here? How would I cope? Would I be pushed to the brink of violent outbursts? Would I succumb to despair? Was there any oasis in this obscure cinder-block desert? All of the memorable excitement of gathering in solidarity with thousands of peace activists at the gates of Fort Benning just down the road faded before the nothingness of my solitary plight in this godforsaken cave of a jail. I prayed for strength and actually began to convince myself that I'd gone through the worst of it when a further disaster hit.

Officer C. had appeared outside with her 'head count' sheet in hand, only to find herself unable to electronically activate the doors. Try as she might, she couldn't pull them open manually either. We heard her call for assistance. Momentarily, two maintenance workers along with a male deputy arrived on the scene and they too failed to fix the electronic malfunction of the doors. Nor could they muster enough muscle power to pry open the heavy metal with their hands.

Those of us inside realized the severity of the situation at once. Our faces flushed in futile desperation. I sensed a barbaric edge of collective panic rising in the day room and hoped to God no one would trigger a stampede. Someone shouted, "Let's go pound on the back door!" Everyone rushed in that direction and began hitting their fists on the locked door. "Hey!" "Hey!" "We want outta here!" Then someone else yelled, "It no good! That door jes' go into another cell block. The lock don't have no key. They not goin' to let us in there. Ain't no way. We be stuck!"

And so it seemed we were indeed stuck. It's bad enough to find yourself locked in a crowded jail; a terrible suffocating sensation envelopes you. Add to this the compelling awareness that not only can you not get out, but no one can get in, even in the event of a violent disturbance. Even in case of a medical emergency. Or a fire. Oddly, an unexpected calm (or was it weariness?) descended upon me and most of the other women. There was nothing we could do. Hours passed us by. Our lunch and our medications were handed to us through the mail slot. The T.V. was off. We ate. We slept.

I was awakened by the sound of keys clinking and rattling at the back door. For at least ten minutes the sound persisted near the key hole. I and a few others approached the door just as we heard a release click and the creaky sound of rusty hinges. Suddenly, the door flew open and Officer C. stood before us like an apparition.

"Hooray!" howled an inmate as another heralded a "Hot damn!" Officer C. stepped into our dismal quarters closing and

Protests and Jails

relocking the door behind her. "I can't allow you into the adjoining cell block, but since y'all have to wait for your own door to get repaired then I'm gonna wait here with you for a while." The grim set of her mouth gave way to a smile and her willingness to remain in our midst caught everyone up into a graced state of surprise.

Officer C. sat herself down at a table in the day room and asked, "Where are the cards? Who's gonna deal the cards?" One of the women who perpetually crouched in her "Heartbreak Hotel" room came forward with a deck and started shuffling. Miss C. commanded, "Y'all go fetch your chips and candy bars, we're gonna take turns playing Five Card Stud like it's goin' outta style." Officer C. was initiating a poker game? Amazing!

She stayed with us for what seemed like a long and generous amount of time, her head bowed over her cards, to shield her hand and maybe as protection for expressions of feelings she could not fully expose before her literally captive companions. I thought she looked almost holy—our very own patron saint of poker.

Right in the middle of her best game, a deputy's voice broke through over Officer C.'s walkie-talkie, ordering her to return to duty at Main Control. I swear I heard her sigh as she set down her cards, but in an instant she recovered herself, reset her posture, stood tall and began her exit toward the back door. She paused briefly and turned to us so that we could hear what she was about to say. "If I have to stay here past midnight, I promise you, that door will be fixed before I go home." She was as good as her word. She stayed on duty until the doors got repaired. Officer C.—the woman I thought had icewater in her veins—did not fail us.

Let each of you look not to your own interests, but to the interests of others.

—Paul to the Philippians 2:4

Opal Takes On The System

Crisp County Jail, Early August 2002

Still waiting to see what happens next, I remain in a cellblock that holds twenty or more women, depending on how many are arrested and booked before others are released. It's all about doing time. Some sleep away the hours, some pace, scream, curse, or cheat at cards to win chocolate bars and sodas purchased at the commissary. Others read books or watch soap operas on T.V. or fold and refold their court papers as if by doing so, they could change their charges or overturn their convictions.

Nobody, however, does time like Opal does time. She's a little bitty skinny young woman with a wide toothy grin, dark skin, cornrowed hair and coal black eyes. She has qualities in her voice that could calm a stormy sea or on another day, set a river raging. She speaks in a dialect used by other Black inmates who, like Opal, are from this region of Georgia. Some of the local women tried to teach me how to feign their accent and speak some colloquial phrases. I failed miserably but my attempts prompted a lot of laughter and in this jail, laughter is a rare commodity. Even Opal laughed.

Opal prays before every meal but doesn't really take more than a bite or two of anything. "Some fool doctor say I got anorexia. I say why eat food when it jus' leave out the other end?" She never joins the rest of us at the table, rather sits alone on her bunk with the food tray on her lap, mostly just moving peas around with her fork or dipping her spoon into and out of her bowl of grits. Fortunately, she drinks bottled water like it's going out of style.

I learned from Opal that she's been incarcerated for a year and proudly earned her GED while behind these bars. She confided that soon she will be transferred to The House (jail talk for State prison) for four more years. It seems she shot her abusive husband in the arm after he had beaten her up for the umpteenth time. I am astonished to learn from her that he remains a man free of any criminal charges.

Late at night, after the main lights are out, Opal faithfully reads scripture passages from the Bible. During the day, she often sits on the edge of her bottom bunk, tracing Greek letters and symbols from the back pages of her Bible onto a tablet. "I never goin home. Never gonna be no man's wife again. I gonna learn Greek. I gonna be a missionary. Make sumpin' of myself. Gonna get outta here."

But days roll in and out of the cellblock like sick snails sliding through mud and Opal is still here, thinner than ever and morose. The mail doesn't get delivered on time. The fan keeps breaking down. Dinner is always cold. We have no clean towels. Slimy water bugs invade the shower stall through the drain. Opal's Bible gets ripped off.

Opal has a rising. She jumps off her bunk with fire in her eyes, grabs her plastic cup and begins banging it against the locked, cage-like door. Bang! Bang! The cup breaks. Opal starts kicking the door with her feet, her arms flapping against her hips.

She wails at the top of her lungs, "I dee-prest! I sad, mad and dee-prest!" She rants and raves, pounds harder on the door and bruises her fists. Instead of her behavior inciting a riot, all the women, including myself, gather in the day room in silence, awe and unspoken solidarity.

Two female guards come to get Opal. She leaves with them wearing a Mona Lisa smile. She never returns. Some whisper, "She in the Hole now". Others guess, "She in the hospital". I think to myself, *Bravo Opal! You are a Greek Goddess! A Missionary on a mission!* But most of the time, we all sit around the table at dinner each evening, repeating what we know is the truth, "Opal got outta here!"

Pentagon Man

Well I woke up this morning with the cold water, with the cold water, with the cold.

—Tom Waits

Each Other's Angels

I took my first trip to Washington D.C. in May of 2000 and quite literally landed flat on my face on a sidewalk at the Pentagon. Along with other SOA Watch protestors, I had volunteered to take part in a non-violent creative re-enactment of a documented Guatemalan massacre at the hands of graduates of the School of the Americas. I was to be one of several 'dead bodies' lying on the ground while others covered us with bloody looking water-soluble soy paint. I felt that my participation in this symbolic gesture at the Pentagon would serve as a way to be in solidarity with the innocent poor who had been murdered throughout Latin America and with their surviving and inconsolable families.

The morning dawned gray, cloudy, dreary and icy cold. But the Pentagon complex—as our 1000 strong group approached it—presented grayer than the sky and far more chilling than the bitter air. The closer we got, the more ominously the stark walls and narrow windows of the Pentagon loomed before us. The bold severity of the massive structure projected an impenetrable sensation of power and I, for one, felt very small in its shadow. This, I realized, is the military eye to the world.

Most of us wore long sleeved shirts and thick sweaters for protection against the inclement weather as we continued processing toward the Pentagon in white death masks with white crosses bearing the names of those massacred in Guatemala as well as in El Salvador and other Central and South American countries. Some in the procession held up familiar names including Oscar Romero, the martyred Jesuits, the slain missionary women, all murdered in El Salvador. Others held up names of simple villagers, men and women, teenagers, children and little babies, whose lives had been torn from them by armed military in other, more remote areas of Latin America.

Our procession culminated at the grassy parade grounds in front of the ceremonial entrance to the Pentagon. Inside, the Joint Chiefs of Staff were no doubt gathering over coffee, anxious to continue outlining war strategies and to begin making decisions about where to next drop bombs in the name of democracy. They most likely had been informed of a group of minor irritants

Protests and Jails

outside—the cluster of non-violent peacemakers making a public statement to close the School of the Americas.

While we protesters rallied and sang near the entrance, a representative of our group made an attempt to enter the Pentagon with the intention of personally presenting to Defense Secretary Bill Cohen, a letter containing evidence of the outrageous deathblows and destruction wreaked upon our poorer neighbors by graduates of the School of the Americas. Needless to say, the representative was refused entry, arrested, and escorted from view in handcuffs.

When we began our theatre drama around mid-morning, I prostrated myself, belly down and silent, on a slab of unforgivingly frigid cement, emulating a victim slain by Guatemalan officers who had been trained how to kill at the SOA. From the ground, I could only see the legs and arms of my fellow resisters who were also sprawled out as though dead. Someone wearing a pair of sneakers approached me and I felt and saw the flow of red paint as it was poured around me and on me.

Soon I heard the swift, hard steps of the Pentagon Police, saw the spit-shine on their shoes as they began arresting and handcuffing those who had been pouring soy paint on us. In the process, one policeman's shiny black shoe stepped on my right hand. It hurt. But I remained still and silent as though dead. Admittedly, I was scared, having no idea what would occur next.

And then it happened. The Pentagon Police gave orders to a group of security assistants to turn high-pressure hoses on those of us who remained on the ground. Not too far from me, I saw one of the assistants kneel down and connect a large black hose to a faucet. A moment later, he turned the nozzle and directed full blasts of water at me. Terrified, I was determined to remain in place. I felt the force of the water as it pounded on me and puddled underneath me. The red paint mixed with water and flooded around me like a bloodbath. Still, I didn't make a move nor did my nearby comrades who were also being hosed. We were deep into the practice of non-violent responsiveness to violence.

Each Other's Angels

After several minutes, I sensed that the security assistant who was still hosing me had grown impatient and upset. Very possibly, he was angry because I was not getting up and moving away from the scene. He began to direct the nozzle at my face. My glasses were washed away while water spilled with a fury into my nose, ears and mouth. The icy cold water amalgamated with icy cold air penetrated my body and I began to shiver uncontrollably. My teeth rattled. My soaked feet were numb. My injured hand was throbbing. I thought to myself, *This is the point where I'm supposed to pray for my enemy,* but I was too overtaken with fear.

I came close to feeling the nightmarish experience of those in Guatemala who had suffered indescribable terror as they were dragged from their dwellings, riddled with bullets, mercilessly murdered at the hands of men with guns. Why? Because they wanted to have a voice, speak truth to power? Because they desired to have a say in their future, yearned for a chance to learn how to read and write and for an opportunity to rise above their oppressed circumstances? My heart ached for every lost soul.

Finally, the security assistant moved his assault of hose water away from me to target more 'bodies'. I was still shivering and felt feverish but a great sense of relief swept over me. Water, unlike bullets, is not fatal. I lifted my head a few inches, in time to see the back of the security man's boots, wet and splattered red, as he walked away. In that moment, for some or other odd reason, I felt a desire to connect with this man, to see his face. I mean, who was he? Did he have a wife? A son who played soccer? A daughter who played with dolls? Did he have a kidney stone or high blood pressure or migraine headaches? Was he a churchgoer? Did he believe that his work at the Pentagon was righteous? Would he drive home pissed off about today's protest, indifferently shrug and try to forget about it when he walked through his door, feel a twinge of shame next time he turned the sprinklers on in his front yard or stepped into his shower?

Ignorant as to the answers to these questions and too weak to get myself up, I whispered, *Holy Mary Mother of God, pray for him now and at the hour of his death.* And I repeated this many times

Protests and Jails

over until at length, friends stepped out of the crowd of witnesses, draped a heavy dry jacket over my shoulders and assisted me to a standing position where I could see a higher view of things.

When they come for the innocent without crossing over your body, cursed be your religion and your life.

—As printed on a Viva House T-shirt

Shannon, Eric, Toni and Elvis

November, 1999, Memphis, Tennessee

Part I: Pilgrimage to Graceland

I've reason to believe, we all will be received, In Graceland

—Paul Simon

In November of the year 1999, my daughter, Shannon—still in her twenties—struck a bargain with me. I would fly with her from LAX to Memphis, Tennessee to visit Graceland and in turn she would travel with me from Memphis to the annual SOA non-violent protest at Fort Benning in Columbus, Georgia. We agreed that it would be fun to bring along our extraverted Catholic Worker friend, Eric, to serve as tour guide and chauffeur. He had already planned on going to the SOA protest and was delighted at the idea of accompanying us on a holiday detour to Elvis Presley territory and then driving us in a rented car to Columbus.

As soon as we landed in Memphis, Eric splendidly integrated his multiple identities as tour guide, chauffeur, newly proclaimed Elvis fan, and peace activist. And that left Shannon and I free to enjoy our mother-daughter holiday. All three of us were provided with beds and warm, southern hospitality by a lovely couple, acquaintances of Eric's and university professors who were active in local peace and justice issues. Shannon and I felt embarrassed about disclosing to them that we were in Memphis for the frivolous purpose of going to Graceland. But then, to our surprise and relief, we noticed a bust of Elvis on the mantelpiece of the professors' living room, right next to framed photos of Gandhi and Martin Luther King.

The evening of our arrival found us holding signs on a street corner downtown, joining our hosts and others in a vigil against the death penalty. Again, I felt uneasy when a couple of people holding anti-death penalty signs asked what brought us here. What else could I say? I confessed that my daughter and I were here to visit Graceland. "Oh! Elvis," one of the ladies declared, "we all love Elvis!" Another lady added convincingly that Elvis had been a peacemaker in his own unique way. "Y'all have a good time at the Mansion tomorrow. And go to Beale Street tonight—you might have an Elvis sighting if you're lucky".

So after the vigil we hit Beale Street. Eric parked the car and we walked a couple of blocks through a heavy evening mist, passing a bridge under which flowed the legendary Mississippi River. Locating a friendly looking restaurant, we went in, sat down and gorged on Southern-style ribs drenched in thick, tangy barbeque sauce and when we felt full, we resumed our tour of Beale Street. Neon lights announced one Blues house after another while evocative sounds of soulful saxophones and bluesy pianos drifted toward us through open doors, encircling us and dancing a slow dance with our senses. Believe it or not, we did catch sight of "Elvis" decked out in a sequined cape with side burns to swoon for, slipping around a corner and disappearing into a dark alley.

Graceland, as we approached it the next morning, appeared smaller in size than the grandiose proportions I had imagined in my mind. The interior of the Mansion was laden with tacky, gaudy, bizarre, extravagant 1950's kitsch. Or as Shannon joyfully exclaimed, "Everything is so Elvis!" We explored all the rooms that were open to tourists and then we strolled around out of doors among shade trees and grazing horses. I myself felt wistful, stepping back in time to a seemingly more innocent era. Eric spoke about the notion of Graceland as a mythical place where, as Paul Simon sings, we all will be received. And Shannon—well Shannon was basking in the glow of a fulfilled dream.

At the end of the trip, we agreed that making a pilgrimage to Graceland was a very quirky way to prepare ourselves for participation in the SOA Protest. Yet it felt really good to balance the deep work of peacemaking awaiting us at Fort Benning in Columbus, Georgia, with a bit of playfulness and a nod to Elvis in Memphis, Tennessee.

Shannon, Eric, Toni and Elvis

November 1999, Columbus, Georgia

Part II: Onward to Fort Benning

The time is always right to do the right thing.

—Martin Luther King Jr.

Shannon is very strong in spirit. However, I've known her to become quiet and subdued in groups, so as she approached the gates of Fort Benning along with Eric and me, I was a bit concerned about her emotional stamina. A crowd of peacemakers, ten thousand strong and full of vitality, had already assembled and were applauding Latin American speakers at the podium on the portable stage, giving testimonies to the suffering they and their families had endured in their countries at the hands of SOA trained officers. Roy Bourgeois spoke about the assassination of Archbishop Oscar Romero by SOA trained men. Singers with guitars hopped on stage and sang hymns and protest songs. To my delight, Shannon conducted herself with poise and grace and applauded every presenter. She also enthusiastically signed up with me for a non-violent training session. I watched her in awe as she listened intently to the trainers who provided the scandalous history of the School of the Americas and then modeled non-violent behavior and non-threatening ways to speak if confronted by police and military staff.

The next morning, after a good night's sleep and a continental breakfast in our nearby hotel, Shannon, Eric and I again joined thousands in a symbolic funeral procession outside the entrance to the military base. Two people on stage at the microphone solemnly read a long list of priests, nuns, teachers, civilian men, women, and children who had died or disappeared over the years in Central and South America at the hands of Latin American military officers trained in the U.S. at Fort Benning's School of the Americas. It had begun to rain and people were shivering with cold but the procession went forward and the crowd replied *Presente!* as each name was read.

Having in previous years, joined the protest against the SOA, I knew there would be a point in the procession where a majority of individuals would turn around and walk back to their starting point while small clusters of prepared groups would walk around the gate, across the property line and onto the military base. As planned, Eric and I began to walk across the line, expecting Shannon to turn around and rejoin the larger group near the stage and podium. However, she proceeded to accompany us onto the base. I felt simultaneously proud and disconcerted because, well, she was an adult making a personal moral decision but she was also my daughter.

We continued walking along a road on the base and after a while the chanting voices of our fellow protesters keeping vigil at the gate began diminishing until at last, we could no longer hear them at all. The rain had stopped altogether and we became wrapped in an unsettling silence deep inside the base. After about ten minutes, we were startled by a man's stern voice—seeming to come through a loud speaker in a nearby tree—identifying himself as a military police officer and warning us that if we didn't return to the outside gate, we would be arrested for trespassing.

Protests and Jails

Eric and I and the others were committed to risking arrest but I urged Shannon to turn around, saying that I respected and admired her for the courage she had already demonstrated just by crossing the line. She stood very still and seemed to be deep in thought. Then she looked at me and said, with a clear and determined voice, "I didn't come all this way, Mom, to turn around and go back." And so, she remained with us as we all knelt down and began singing *Amazing Grace* while one after another, we were handcuffed by members of the military police and put on one of two buses that had pulled up behind us. The whole lot of us—maybe 40 people—were driven further onto the base and confined inside a big tent with a supply of drinking water on a fold-out table and a couple of portable toilets just outside.

For several hours we were each fingerprinted and given a paper, namely a 'Ban and Bar' stipulating that we were not allowed to re-enter the base for a period of five years. After that, the M.P.'s loaded us into the buses again and drove us to a park about two miles away from the vigil. It was quite a memorable walk back for us as we paraded through neighborhoods where residents waited in their front yards for us, waving and offering cookies and lemonade.

Some mothers bond with their daughters by getting manicures and pedicures together or by curling up on a sofa watching old episodes of *Friends* on TV. And those are OK things to share. But nothing can rival the bonding that Shannon and I experienced that year by accompanying each other to Graceland in Memphis Tennessee and following it up with a trip to Fort Benning, Georgia where we sang Amazing Grace while getting arrested for doing "the right thing".

Shannon Faces Chemo and Joanne Meets the Judge

The Catholic Agitator, March 8, 2014

Where is the way to the dwelling of light . . . ?

—Job 38:19

Each Other's Angels

Life always waits for some crisis to occur before revealing itself at its most brilliant.

—Paulo Coelho

My daughter, Shannon, has stage 2 breast cancer. She had the misfortune of inheriting her grandmother's and her father's BRACA 2 genetic mutation. So now, Shannon's facing her third round with this unpredictable, vitriolic disease having already survived cervical and ovarian cancer. I (along with her husband, Joe and sister, Heather) serve as her transportation team, alternately accompanying her while she braves four months of chemotherapy. David and Mark, her brothers, along with their wives and Heather's husband, are tremendously supportive via texts, cards and phone calls. Thank God for family who show up in hard times. When the seemingly endless chemo ordeal is finally over, I've volunteered to be at Shannon's bedside after her double mastectomy, changing her bandages and hoping, praying for positive outcomes.

Meanwhile, my retirement from County Mental Health is almost a year away. That means that for several more months, I'll be assisting men and women suffering from mental illness, drug addiction and alcoholism as they leave jail and try to figure out how to reconstruct their shattered lives. For over 30 years, in one way or another, I've been walking with people like the ones I accompany now, as they languish on the streets or dance the bureaucratic boogey in and out of jails, social service centers, soup kitchens and shelters. I point the way and I walk by their side, again praying for positive outcomes.

The problem is, I'm weary. The people at the jail are too damaged—or maybe it's that I feel too exhausted to hold wounded souls by the hand for much longer. My daughter is too young to die and I feel too old to even consider surviving that sort of unthinkable loss as a mother. It's a dark time for me right now. And I'm scared. Even with glasses, I can barely see the light of day that Bruce Springsteen's song assures us is just around the corner. Of

Protests and Jails

course, life is not really an *all about me* affair is it? I'm constantly reminding myself to avoid the false perception that when I help others it's *all about me* being generous. Really it's all about love, isn't it?

Yet, like I said, I'm weary. I'm tired. And I'm scared of the shadow of loneliness. In Act I of Samuel Beckett's *Waiting For Godot*, Estragon proclaims, "I can't go on." To which Vladimir replies, "That's what *you* think." How do I reach that place of surrender where I can more easily acknowledge that I'm part of a larger community, part of the family of humanity, one of God's countless children? That indeed, it is *not* about me alone, it's about *us*. It's not only about *my* struggle with exhaustion, *my* fear of the dark. It's about recognizing the weariness and the fear of darkness in everyone around me. And, in the end, it's about all of us helping each other to go on even when we feel the fatigue of self-defeat. It's about reaching out.

Last Tuesday morning found me reaching out at the local county courthouse. One of the women I visit at the jail was going to be sentenced. What never ceases to surprise me when I enter the courtroom is how much it resembles a city cathedral. The judge's podium serves as the altar. He is the high priest of the day. On the wall behind the podium, the Great Seal of California hangs in lieu of a stained glass window. (In actuality, the courtroom is windowless). And below the Seal, an American flag hangs much like a crucifix on a pageant pole. Twenty-two lights, patterned in a perfect circle on the ceiling, glow in the fluorescent fashion of a fallen angel's halo.

We, the people, sit outside the rails, in neat rows, some distance from the judge. They, the charged and the guilty as charged, sit inside the rails, to the left of the judge, resembling penitent, voiceless choir members in handcuffs and ankle chains. Directly in front of the judge, sit the lawyers—much like altar servers. Some always seem distracted and unprepared while others I know to be sincere and dedicated, their ideals intact, their skills honed for the sake of those who are otherwise least represented (To be fair, I also know a few judges who are as upright and compassionate as the tangled web of the criminal justice system allows).

When I first arrived on this particular Tuesday, the judge's seat was still empty. Deputies were chatting with the court reporter. The public defender was in cautious conversation with the district attorney. Five minutes later, the judge walked through a door that opens closest to his podium. All rose to their feet as he entered. A hush fell over the entire space as he sat down and—much in the manner of a demigod—grabbed his gavel, tapped it and proclaimed court to be in session.

I took a moment to contemplate clothing. The judge was draped in a long, black robe, lawyers in expensive grey suits, deputies in starched green uniforms, the court recorder donned a perfectly fitted navy blue silk dress while in-mates wore orange crumpled cotton jumpsuits. Most of the rest of us—the congregation so to speak—were garbed in a variety of street clothes, guys in faded jeans and stained t-shirts, women in sheer blouses and skin tight leggings, a few of us in dresses or slacks and jackets. The clothes in the courtroom on both sides of the rail revealed a lot. To my mind, they exposed a modern day caste system.

The day progressed and the ceremonials did, oddly, resemble a Mass. The Word of the Law was proclaimed. Woe-to-you was the over riding theme as one by one, the in-mates were sentenced for their mostly drug related, non-violent mistakes. Ten days in jail with three years probation. Three years in jail with no probation. Six months in jail followed by a mandatory six months of residential rehabilitation. Once in a while, for some lucky man or woman, the judge and the attorneys distributed what passed for merciful justice. Others were shown very little mercy by the court and were forced to listen to sermons that stung like bullets. Everyone in the room knew that there would be no banquet at this Mass. It was strictly a sacrificial gig.

After a break, Joanne, the woman I was working with, appeared before the judge. She stood up, thin, pale and powerless. The public defender called me to the rail and the judge allowed me to speak on Joanne's behalf. "Your Honor, I have secured a bed

Protests and Jails

for this young woman" I reported in my most professional voice, "at a sober house. And I have funding to cover the cost. I can pick her up in a county car and transport her there tomorrow if she is released." The judge paused, scowling. A moment later it was clear to me that he was in a contrary mood and he sentenced Joanne back to jail for thirty days.

Joanne just stood there with her mouth agape, defeated in the dust of his decision, denied Communion at the altar. She and I both knew that the judge's decree would result in her losing the reserved bed at the sober house. I recalled a quote by Robertson G. Ingerson: "Wait until the chains are broken, until dungeons are not regarded as temples before you write a creed." And suddenly my eyes were pealed and I no longer viewed the courtroom as a cathedral.

With a disappointing Tuesday behind me, I took Wednesday off work so that I could drive Shannon to chemotherapy. She hopped into my car wearing a cute, colorful "chemo cap" that presented more like a stylish turban. Her head underneath the cap was completely bald and she had no eyebrows except for what she penciled on. I complemented her on still having eyelashes. "They're fake." She said this matter-of-factly with a hint of humor. She confessed that it wasn't pleasant when she talked because she had sores in her mouth. My lovely daughter! I wished so hard that I could trade places with her! And I knew that I would have wholeheartedly thanked God had my wish been granted on the spot.

In contrast to the courtroom suggesting a downtown cathedral, the cancer center reminded me of a large modern parish in an affluent neighborhood. Situated across from a Catholic hospital, the building complex and the surrounding landscape possessed a quality of sacredness. I'm reluctant to add that it's the sort of sacred space that only money, lots of money, creates. The outside walls are painted in muted, natural hues. Ferns and fruitless olive trees and a variety of eco friendly shrubs offer beauty and life. Inside are live green potted plants, pastel walls and smiles on the faces of cheerful, mostly young, medical staff.

Each Other's Angels

In the waiting room, I reflected on the profit making elements of healing centers and on the injustices that abound when people get sick and seek treatment. However, I soon changed the direction of my thoughts because I was landing hard on the pinpoint of a personal paradox . . . Shannon needed this place! Her life literally depended on the doctors and nurses inside the facility. So I consciously chose *not* to include this beautiful center as part of a medical/pharmaceutical system run amok. Even so, one burning question managed to break into and enter my head, robbing me of peace and quiet in the waiting room . . . is this a good place or a bad place?

When we entered the actual chemo room, it felt as though the expensively adorned parish church had morphed into a monastery where strangers are welcomed like Christ and the sick are tenderly tended. The room felt round because of the island in the middle that serves as the nurse's station. And the nurses must have all been Mother Teresa's nieces and nephews. They were kind and skilled, attentive and uplifting. Situated against all four walls were about twenty leather lounge chairs, each with an intravenous drip catheter hanging from a pole with wheels on the base. Every lounge chair had a window behind it with an outside view. The whole place was filled with soft sunshine rays like the ones that emanated from my childhood holy cards.

However, shadows and reality soon crept into the monastic setting. A nurse 'hooked' Shannon up and the chemo cocktail—a poignantly necessary poison that kills cancer cells but also destroys healthy cells, compromises the immune system, and wreaks havoc on the body—began to flow from the bag and through the tubing that connects the catheter to the portal inserted near Shannon's shoulder. On it flowed, invading her bloodstream—a lesser evil on its way to hopefully overcome a greater evil. Jesus healed people by touching and gazing, with spittle and prayer. He never used poison as a cure. Where was Jesus now when my daughter needed him most? *God, please be stronger than my doubts and disbelief. God, please be bigger than any and all humanly designed systems.*

God, please be kinder than chemo. These were my ruminations, my mantras.

During the final hour, we sat silently, sifting through magazines, Shannon on her lounge chair and me on a wooden chair. "Sit in your cell as in Paradise.," advised the Eleventh Century monk, St. Romuald, "Sit waiting, content with the Grace of God." But this place was no monk's cell nor was it heaven. How could I wait patiently as in Paradise knowing that a ticking time bomb called cancer was lodged inside my daughter's body? And no. I was not able to sit content. I knew how nauseated Shannon would become, how her bones would ache and how everything she would try to eat and drink would be tainted a metallic taste. I wanted this over. Now. Remarkably, it was Shannon who demonstrated patience and a grounded sort of calm. It was Shannon who smiled in the face of fear. Who said thank you when the nurse brought her a bottle of water. She was for me, a tangible sign of the Grace of God.

So. Yes. I'm weary, tired, exhausted. And scared. So I assume, is Joanne. So, I know, is Shannon. Suffering and accompanying suffering depletes us and eventually we begin to sense that the whole planet is overwhelmed with fatigue and may soon be overtaken altogether by indifferent or corrupt systems. I believe there are antidotes, if not to suffering then to despair. And the antidotes are these: Faith, hope and love . . . not in the abstract because virtues are not intended to remain merely noble notions admired from afar like expensive vases. I strive to embrace these virtues passionately, as living entities, and then release them into the world to animate the lives of others.

Through faith, we dive head long into the darkness. Through hope, we imagine previously unimaginable blessings. Through love, we strive to offer our hearts to those who cross our paths, to bend down and lift up the fallen and slow down for those who are hobbling behind on worn out legs; to wrap our aching arms around other aching arms; to share provisions with those who are poor and hungry, to visit the sick and the imprisoned, tend the dying and honor the dead. We rest when our own bodies need resting, we pray when our own souls need restoring. We forgive others and ourselves for messing up. We remember how important it is to laugh, cry, dance and sing joyfully—to feel our humanness. We repeat these acts again and again and yet again until justice kisses mercy and jails are emptied and cancer is cured. We do this until we become Light.

Then shall your light break forth like the dawn and your healing shall spring up speedily; your righteousness shall go before you; the glory of the Lord shall accompany you.
—Proverbs 20:27

(Note: Joanne is still searching for light. Shannon successfully completed her treatments and surgeries.)

Sister Louise

Crisp County jail, August 11, 2002

Outside my cell window, above chain link fencing and rolls of razor wire, the sky is an expanse of cornflower blue, interrupted here and there with clusters of billowy white clouds. Inside, everything is somber and lackluster. This day, Sunday, August 11th, marks the end of the first month of my six-month prison sentence, having spent the first week in the dingy, dungeon-like confines of Muscogee County Jail, followed by two weeks in a cleaner, more modernized Harris County Jail and this past week in a crowded cellblock of Crisp County Jail.

The full-flowered notion I initially carried within me—that I would serve time with spirit-filled stamina, enduring hardships with faith in the idea of furthering justice—has begun to wilt. The fact that I am blessed with an outside support system of solid non-violent peace activists is at present offering me little consolation after enduring these thirty long days in the state of Georgia behind bars. Five more months to go and I'm already worn down and weary. I know that there is more to me than mere wimpiness but

Protests and Jails

confinement has inclined my mind toward the negative aspects of myself and my circumstances.

Last night I couldn't sleep because after 11:00 PM lights out, some of the women in my cellblock began quarreling and screaming with a fierceness that unsettled the marrow in my bones. By 2:00 AM things quieted down and efforts to read a book by flashlight failed because I was too tired to focus on the pages. I eventually dozed off for about a couple of hours but that brief snooze perversely added a layer of fatigue to my already sleep deprived body.

This morning after breakfast, still feeling sleepy, I sign up for a Southern Baptist version of 'church', one of the few extracurricular activities an inmate can request and easily receive approval for from the jail staff. I confess my purpose is not so much about holiness than it is to take advantage of an opportunity to leave the monotony of my cell and stretch my legs by walking to the scheduled bible service in the library room at the end of the hall. On the way out, I bump my head on the bunk frame and glance sourly at it as though it were an animate creature set on harming me. My already murky mood darkens.

I walk behind several other women along a drafty corridor and into the unkempt and sparsely book-lined library, converted for the day into a makeshift chapel. As do the other inmates, I sit myself down on one of the metal folding chairs that flank a rectangular table. Before long, a subtle fragrance, hinting of far eastern spices, drifts into the room, followed by the elegant entrance of Sister—meaning a sister of the Lord—Louise. She stands before us, a tall, beautiful, Black woman; strong-boned, straight-backed, broad-shouldered and dignified, yet also warm and inviting like her perfume. No doubt, she possesses both substance and grace.

Sister Louise pauses for a moment before taking her place, and I notice her dark, even-toned flawless complexion and how impeccably she has smoothed her hair back off her face, securing it with an opaque ribbon. The other thing I observe is how Sister Louise shimmers. All over. Aside from her black crepe dress and black patent leather heels, she is draped in glistening golden hues. A sheer yellow scarf floats around her neck, cascades down her shoulders, and on it, embroidered in gold glitter, are the words *Jesus Loves You.* Her ears, wrists, and fingers are ornamented with fine gold jewelry. Even her nails are painted with golden polish, matching the shade of her frosted lipstick. As if this isn't enough, Sister Louise is blessed with hazel eyes that shine like twin bronze sunsets–they are the kind of eyes you want to look into because you'd swear they illuminate some sort of hidden message meant just for you.

Sister Louise is inviting us to stand up with her. Our chairs clatter as we rise. Sister Louise starts things off with a handclap and a gospel cry, *Come Lord Jesus!* Her eyes ignite and begin rotating around beneath long, fluttering lashes. Her face is flushed with sudden emotion. She is carried away. Whatever has taken hold of her is contagious. Soon the room is full of praising prophets—hand-clapping, eye-rolling, crying, swaying, swooning, Black women—glory-glorifying the Lord in ways completely unfamiliar to the constraints of my more subdued white Catholic upbringing.

I am beside myself with sheepish embarrassment. I don't know how to behave or not behave. I close my eyes as though doing so might render me invisible, might carry me away from this jail, out of Georgia, back to the quiet Benedictine monastery near my California desert home where praying is refined and predictable, expressed in the form of solemn chants interspersed with meditative moments of silence . A slow panic begins to creep over me but is mercifully diffused as someone affectionately pats me on the back.

Soon, the singing begins. Voices resound and resonate, rise and fall, with ecstatic strength and unhampered purity. The robust singing surprisingly calms me to the core. *I say yes, Lord,* the women sing and clap their hands harmonizing effortlessly, their traditional Southern Baptist gospel intonations bounding off the walls. *I say yes! To your Will and to your Way. I say yes . . . I say yes.* A joyful sensation washes over me and I feel cleansed, my spirit bathing in the rhythm, lyrics and melody of the song.

A hushed quiet sweeps the room as the singing subsides. We all sit. Sister Louise reads from Psalm 27: *The Lord is my light and my salvation, whom shall I fear?* She then proceeds to speak, her phrases dropping like honey from a spoon, glistening in the globe of my imagination like the gold adorning her body. I lean on every word. No, I *fall* into every word—words of comfort, caution, consolation; words of hope, words of wisdom. Words that break into the shadows of this caged netherworld where injustices abound and indignities humiliate body and soul in countless forms. Words that pour upon the hard-luck women of Georgia like balm in Gilead, soothing their open wounds and broken dreams, and soothing me as well.

And now, Sister Louise is asking, "Who in this room needs Saving?" No one volunteers, so she softly circles around the room, gently touching each and every one of us. Some women begin to weep. I begin to breathe deep full breaths as though I have just tasted air for the first time. A young woman decides to give a testimony—raw and stinging with the truth of her mistakes and mishaps. I marvel at her forthrightness.

Next thing I know, Sister Louise is looking right at me with her deep, bronze, liquid eyes and she invites me to tell her my name. I whisper, "Toni". "And what is *your* testimony, child?" For a moment, I'm stunned and self-conscious. Then, to my own amazement, I begin to share my story—how I try to practice non-violence; how I travelled to Georgia from my home in California and took part in a protest against a U.S. military school that teaches torture and terror tactics to Latin American officers right here at Fort Benning; how I was tried and sentenced in a Federal court of law along with fellow peace activists. I confide how difficult it is to be locked up so far away from home, family, and friends. I admit that I miss the familiarity of Catholic Mass and the option of receiving Communion. And thank you, Sister Louise I say, and thank you everyone, I say, for accepting me, the stranger in your midst.

The room is swirling. I believe it is swirling with grace. Ebony skinned prisoners and golden-clad Sister Louise circle around me. They all seem so vibrant with the richness of the moment whereas I feel pale and besieged with nervous tension. I find myself blurting out, "I hope you don't want to save me . . . I've already been saved at the Muscogee County Jail during a revival service." Which is true, I remind myself. "Toni, child," says Sister Louise, "we'd just like to invite you to offer us a closing prayer. That's all, honey."

Feeling inadequate at voicing spontaneous prayers in the presence of others, I am tempted to refuse. But an honest sense of humility envelopes me and I begin. I pray for the women in here and for all women in captivity everywhere. I pray for Sister Louise and for all who minister in jails and prisons. I pray for peace on earth and for the conversion of hearts. "Glory!" proclaim the women. "Umm-Hmm," they mutter. "Praise Jesus," they cry. "Hallelujah, sister!" they conclude. As I say the final "Amen," my soul fills with gratitude; my eyes perceive a certain slant of scattered light filtering into the room. "It's the overhead light fixture come on unexpectedly," explains a woman. But I know better.

Stranger In The Night

Crisp County Jail, December, 2002

Come to this corner tonight at seven o'clock. Jesus has a message just for you.

—Carson McCullers, *The Heart Is A Lonely Hunter*

It's a dark evening in Advent. Everything—every event, every observation, every thought, every prayer, is reduced to smallness. There are no big stories for me to tell from this insulated bordered land upon which I have been existing since last summer. I remain locked away in this jail, invisible to the rest of the world, confined to my cell, segregated from all other prisoners with the exception of my cellmate, for twenty-three out of twenty-four hours of each day.

The destinations to which I am escorted during my one hour "out" vary according to a loosely enforced schedule and what seems to be the convenience of the jail staff. Some days I'm taken to the courtyard where I walk round and round. Other days, it could be to the library, the visitation room, the chapel, the doctor's in-house office.

No matter, the smallness follows me wherever I go in here, especially through the corridors—long and narrow—that lead both captives and captors from one place to another. I'm tempted to convince myself of the hauntedness of these halls, but of course it's not specters I see when I'm marched past the lines of metal doors dotted with face-grills. The shadowy figures inside are human and as alive as you can be in imprisonment.

Earlier this evening, I was escorted to the jail clinic for a medication review. A correctional officer commanded me to stand against the wall across from the clinic entrance and to keep quiet. I did what I was told. That's when I saw him, silent and alone, in the corner opposite me. An old man, tethered to a rickety, outdated wheelchair. He was holding his catheter bag, half-full of blood-tinged urine, leaking through the tubing onto the left pant leg of his torn orange jumpsuit. His breathing was labored and he coughed sporadically, spitting phlegm into a soiled cloth he clenched between bony fingers.

The man, rather than meeting my eyes, gazed beyond me without expression, into the nihility of the cream-colored corridor. He bore a bent, pained posture, the few thin remnants of gray hair clinging to his scalp announcing the last vestiges of vitality. The whole sorry image brushed across my heart much in the way a wounded bird's shattered wing might graze a window.

I supposed to myself that he'd failed to pay a fine of some sort or wrote bad checks to cover rent. It otherwise seemed implausible that such a depressed and physically incapacitated man could have found the strength or even the will to commit a violation meriting a jail term. Yet here he was before me, his creased and weather-torn face devoid of joy, his watery eyes conveying nothing.

In a few weeks it would be Christmas and I had an unreasonable urge to run up, embrace that man of sorrow and whisper in his ear, *Get ready for the Birth!* I wanted to reshape his history, lead him to a previous, more fortunate day in his life where the sun shone upon him like a great promise. I longed to peel away the years from his fractured body, his battered countenance, his ghostly spirit. I wished that I could accompany him back to the promise of his youth, where he could stand tall and and unblemished on strong limbs, with glossy black curls crowning his head and a straight brow dignifying his forehead. I'd say, *This—and not this—will be your destiny. Make a lie of your downfall! Go here and not there. You don't have to live the small life inside a jail. Quick! Take a different turn on the path.*

But nothing came of my imaginings. An hour passed and I was still waiting to see the doctor and so was my tormented friend in the wheelchair. We waited and waited. An unspoken awareness of each other transacted although we never exchanged a word out loud. What an odd pair—the restless peace activist and the crippled criminal. By the time a nurse appeared to wheel the old man inside, his catheter bag was full. He reeked of urine and humiliation. I hoped to God he didn't feel too small, as I felt for not having conjured the magical power to lead him back to a better place in time where he could begin again.

Alone now, my back aching against the wall, my legs sore from standing too long, I reflected on Advent. On the slowness of things. On how being a prisoner is all about waiting. Waiting for court, for one more day to end, for release. Our waiting is done behind locked doors and we are mere apostrophes to the times. Outside, big things are dominating societies. Violence explodes in places near and far. Blind ambition and unleashed greed manipulate the order of things. Wheels turn and deals are made in private jets flying above cities or more likely, in opulent office suites boasting private bars stocked with expensive liquors and Cuban cigars. Elsewhere, shops overflow with a wealth of merchandise while green and red holiday neon signs subliminally seduce shoppers to open their wallets. Buy Everything! Buy Now! 'Tis the season . . .

I tell myself that I don't want any part of big events. Yet I can't say that I relish the complete defeat of smallness. And certainly the man in the wheelchair did not set out to fulfill a destiny of brokeness. Then again, if Jesus were to show up this Christmas in the guise of a wronged gladiator, armored, ruthless, seeking revenge, smashing evil empires without discretion, throwing corporate heads, misguided politicians, hypocritical religionists, and warriors on all sides into the proverbial lions den, how would any of us find our way to grace and goodness?

I trust that Jesus will *not* show up this Christmas ready to do bloody battles in the fashion of Big Screen movie stars like Sylvester Stallone and Russell Crowe. Jesus knows how to enter this wounded world. He knows how to enter this jail. No doubt he will be born to us once again, small, vulnerable, and despised by those in power who see his birth as a threat to their authority. He will keep entering into our world in this humble way until we ourselves learn to respect and love, protect and nurture all among us who are also small, vulnerable, and despised.

The nurse comes out to take me in. She smiles. It is a little smile. I accept it without question.

The MPO

Crisp County Jail, 2002

I peek out of the narrow vertical slit of glass that serves as my cell window. It's morning and I gratefully soak in the slender view of wet green grass, imagining the rich scent of blooming trees barely visible just beyond the jail parking lot.

A wild bird, no larger than my palm, flutters into view, skillfully perches itself at eye-level onto a portion of the wire fence that surrounds the correctional facility, avoiding the twisted barbs that could easily tear its wings. We both pause and become still, our eyes sizing each other up—the free bird and the caged woman. Soon, the sky beckons and the bird takes flight. I press my nose to the glass, fogging a small circular portion of the window with an outbreath, feeling envious that I too cannot fly away.

Surrender is not a practice that comes easy to me. Nor does the sensation of being brought level with the frailer aspects of common humanity. Yet I must surrender to my situation and I am in this moment feeling frail. I leave the window and lie on my bunk remembering the Sunday afternoon at the SOA protest last November outside the gates of Fort Benning here in Georgia. It was a day of reverence and a day of reckoning. Everything was glorious and we processed ten thousand strong, solemnly chanting the names of the dead and disappeared from Central and South America who suffered at the hands of SOA graduates, responding to each name with *PRESENTE*.

We formed a non-violent force, speaking truth to power, giving voice to the voiceless. Together, we pleaded—demanded—that the men with guns, the U.S. officers who train them, the U.S. government that encourages and sustains the violence with our tax dollars, stop the madness and close the School of the Americas (currently known as the Western Hemispheric Institute for Security Cooperation).

My own heart that day was pounding with exhilaration as I managed my way around a fence and proceeded onto military property. There, I joined hands with a Franciscan priest and over 35 other peaceful demonstrators. We walked further onto the Base until we could no longer hear the singing at the gate. A voice boomed out over a speaker system, warning us that we were about to be arrested for trespassing. We knelt down. We began to sing an old freedom song, "We Shall Overcome". A swarm of military police descended and I found myself separated by a few yards from the others, obeying a command to lie belly-flat on the ground while damp leaves infiltrated my nostrels and dirt seeped into my mouth.

While my face remained down, a young, burly MPO—military police officer—approached me and roughly handcuffed my wrists behind my back. The handcuffs were plastic but nonetheless they were so tight it felt as though I had no blood flow to my hands. As my throbbing fingers began to swell, a wild panic flooded my body, invaded my head, and I felt aflame with fear. My initial impulse was to scream, resist and defy my captor—an awful temptation for a practitioner of non-violence. So, instead, I attempted to control my breathing in order to calm myself down.

Protests and Jails

With each breath I made efforts to calm myself by contemplating the Catholic Worker house where I reside, situated in the High Desert region of Southern California, near a Benedictine Abbey. I began recalling the peace of the monastery where I found strength and solace resting, walking, working in the ceramics shop, attending Mass, sharing in the meals, and praying along with the monks. And I began reminding myself how, in the early days of monasticism, the monks, after chanting a psalm, would fall into silent prostration, freely and willingly remaining flat on the ground of the chapel for the same measurement of time that it took them to pray the preceding psalm.

It occurred to me, as I lay pronated and shackled, that I might adapt a version of sacred prostration to my own situation. I began to recite out loud a rather skewed version of the Catholic Litany of Saints. *Saint Anthony. Pray for us. Saint Paul. Pray for us. Saint Peter. Pray for us.* Call it grace. Call it Divine Intervention. Call it plain old luck. The recitation began to release me from all anxiety and fear. *Our Lady of Guadalupe. Pray for us. Saint John the Baptist. Pray for us.* As my recitations went on, the MPO walked over to me, bent down and inexplicably loosened my handcuffs and utterly surprised me with a few reassuring words saying "You'll be alright. Just keep praying." So I continued, *Saint John of the Cross. Pray for us. Saint Joseph. Pray for us.*

After a few more saints were evoked, the MPO pulled me upright. I was still praying, *Mother Teresa. Pray for us. Oscar Romero. Pray for us. Dorothy Day. Pray for us.* A single leaf dangled from my chin. I crunched on a piece of muddy soil. The officer led me to a bus. It was full of my fellow peace pilgrims. They were belting out what must have been the hundredth chorus of "We Shall Overcome." It was indeed going to be alright.

Here in the jail where I'm now confined, I pray regularly for the MPO who offered me a fleeting moment of consideration. I'm no longer in the town where he is stationed and I'm three thousand miles away from the Abbey but I continue with my monastic prayer life, however clumsy and faulty it may be.

Each Other's Angels

For brief periods in the mornings and evenings I lay on my stomach on my bunk, reading the psalms from a tattered paperback psalmody, pausing silently after each one in the fashion of an ancient Desert Mother. Into those pauses I bring to mind the MPO, the victims of the SOA, their perpetrators, their surviving families, my own family members, my friends, the women I've met in the jails, the SOAWatch organizers, my fellow peace activists, our attorney and his team, our supporters, the judge who sentenced us, the U.S. marshals who transport us, the county and federal correctional officers, the local sheriff, and the Benedictine monks who taught me by example how to practice the ancient, sacred art of spiritual surrender to a loving God.

I am discovering pathways to an inner sense of liberation through prayer much in the way the wild bird I just viewed through my prison window maneuvered its feathered body through barbed wire unharmed and spread its wings and flew into freedom.

The Lord saved them from distress . . . brought them out of darkness and deepest gloom and broke away their chains.

—Psalm 107

The Screaming Man

Crisp Co, Jail, August 26, 2002

A couple of hours ago while I was reading a book on my bunk, a male inmate, somewhere down the long and desolate main corridor of the jail, began to scream. His haunting wail pierced my ears although I could see nothing since the steel entrance door to my cell stays shut and locked day and night. I could, however, hear the pain, anger and desperation in his voice as it echoed off the walls and seeped through the half opened metal flap of the food, medication, and mail slot located in the day room area of the cell. Next came a succession of stern, commanding voices tangling with the guttural pleas of the screaming man, followed by an unsettling quiet like the calm before a storm.

I had no time to ponder on reasons for the man's anguished outcry for within a minute or two, strong gusts of air began to noisily whirl through the cell's air vents, startling me as well as my cellmate, Kaya. Then in an instant, just as I put a supportive arm over Kaya's shoulder, the forced air became virulent, filling our day room with an odor both nasty and noxious. Our eyes stung and reddened while tears flowed down our flushed cheeks and we began coughing uncontrollably. I felt a gripping tightness in my chest and fire in my throat. The atmosphere in our room was toxic. I let go of Kaya and wrapped my fingers around my neck, terrified I might be gasping my final breaths on earth.

Running to the intercom and pressing the button, my voice failed me utterly. My constricted vocal chords were so damaged that all I could do was issue a throaty "Help! Get us out of here!" Someone retorted in an official sounding manner, "You can't come out. We used pepper spray to extract someone from another cell. All the air vents are linked so we're blasting air and you'll just have to wait until everything clears up." My initial panic turned to outrage. Pounding on the metal door, wasting my precious breath, I ridiculously ranted about cruel and unusual punishment in a raspy whisper that no one could hear.

Kaya regained her composure before I did mine. She soaked our towels in cold running water, wrung them, and placed one over my face and one over her face. It relieved us to a slight degree. About 15 minutes passed before the fumes dissipated enough that we could breathe somewhat normally. Later, a nurse opened our slot and handed us our prescription medications. She was wearing a facemask. She did not offer any such antidote to us. I asked her if the man who had been screaming was all right and were people other nearby cells all right? She flatly replied that it was none of my business.

Resting later on my bunk, I pondered on the plight of the screaming man. And I confronted my own contradictions in the face of the injustices that had occurred today as well as on other days inside this facility. One day last week, I did a 24-hour juice fast in the interest of world peace and the next morning I slurped down cold grits and scrambled eggs and hoarded my sugar packets. Some days I write poems of liberation and sonnets of love, other days I curl up like a ball of discarded yarn and cry myself to sleep. One minute, I reach out to comfort Kaya and the next, I am paralyzed with fear and she reaches out to me with a cold, wet cloth.

There's no denying that doing time in here is a great equalizer. One man's screams affect all of us and we are bowed low before those who have keys and authority over us. And really, it makes little difference whether the air is fair or foul, it's hard to breathe deep and overcome the suffocating experience of jail life. Sometimes God seems to have forgotten us in the hiddenness of our captivity. I suppose that my challenge is to continually hand my fears and doubts over to God even when I don't feel the presence of a Higher Power.

Waiting in the Belly of the Beast for My Grandson's Birth

Crisp County Jail, October, 2002

Then Jonah prayed to the Lord his God from the belly of a great fish . . .

—Book of Jonah, Chapter 2

It's raining. A downpour. My ears are brimming with ominous sounds of thunder. Lightening flashes outside while overhead, fluorescent lamps flicker. I'm still in Georgia, still in jail. Water is falling hard on the rooftop, I'm homesick and in a funk.

On the other side of the country in California, almost 3,000 miles away from this jail cell, my son, Mark and his wife Susan, are most likely at this very minute putting finishing touches on a baby nursery. I sense their joyful anticipation as they prepare for the birth of their infant son. And I know that my own melancholy streams from the fact that I will be absent for the birth of my first grandchild.

A profound sense of my own powerlessness pervades my spirit. Much like Jonah, my initial plea to God is for personal deliverance. This is the third Georgia county jail I've been in since beginning my six—month descent through the criminal justice system as a prisoner of conscience and I'm still devastated from news that I will not be transferred to a minimum—security facility in California as I had initially anticipated. Such a move would have brought me in closer proximity to my family and allotted me more freedom of movement and time outdoors. I confess that the prayer that begins "Take, Lord, receive, all my liberty . . . " is one I've yet to pray with conviction.

All three of the county jails have kept me in lock—down situations, meaning that I have remained locked inside of cells with extremely limited access to an outdoor yard or a library or anything else beyond the walls of my confinement. For purposes of my own dark amusement, I've divided the jails into categories based on the degrees of over—crowding, bad food, poor hygiene, safety conditions, visitation privileges and access to outside supportive services. Muscogee County Jail—hell; Harris County Jail—oasis; Crisp County Jail—purgatory. In traditional Catholic terms, purgatory is a temporary place of discomfort and purification wherein a soul is transported after death to be purged of impurities and through some sort of mystical alchemy, made ready to bear the Light of God's Face. There you have it.

The Old Testament story of Jonah and the Whale infers that periods of purgation are also often required while a person is still alive on this earth—an especially effective process if one is reluctant to take on the burdens (and privileges) of a prophet. I pause here and chuckle. Me? A prophet? If so, I'm an extremely reluctant one. But then, so it seems, was Jonah.

Certainly I'm swallowed up; traveling down, belly flopping around inside of this dismal detention center. And with great discomfort, I realize that the growling, dank, stomach of a giant fish couldn't be much worse than the cramped quarters of my dreary cell. Finding myself locked up for 23 out of every 24 hours each day is a whale of a challenge (notice the pun). Moment after moment, I'm tempted to whine and scream in the discourteous manner of a minor prophet, foretelling only doom, gloom, and despair.

"I called to the Lord out of distress," Jonah tells us, "and the Lord delivered me." Even as I note this, I sense God's answer to my own similar circumstances: *This is not about you alone, Toni!* Can it be that grace is as precipitous as rain? I ask this because my thoughts are suddenly awash with concerns much broader in scope than my own personal problems. Awareness descends upon me that the whole wounded world is crying out for deliverance. And I remind myself that I'm imprisoned because I freely chose to risk arrest by participating in a peaceful protest at the School of the Americas.

Could coming to terms with these sorts of realizations be how a prophet grows up? I begin to pray prayers of intercession.

> God, I pray for President Bush, that he refrain from beating war drums against Iraq; for the people of Iraq who, already on their knees from the effects of sanctions, must now suffer the deadly aim of bombs; for the closing of the School of the Americas behind whose shameful doors torture and terror techniques are still taught; for the poor who are still poor, the homeless who are still homeless, the hungry who are still hungry, the violent who are still violent; for prisoners everywhere—alone, despised and dismissed by retributive societies; for the soul of the Pentagon whose commanders insist on global war making and nuclearizing the heavens; for our earth as it groans under the strain of environmental abuse.

A mature prophet, I remind myself, not only remembers to pray for existing circumstances but cries out for change, atonement, a new order more aligned with the all—encompassing heart of God. Little by little, I'm getting there despite temptations to focus on life through the shallow lens of self-preservation. If God indeed brought me to this particular jail for the purpose of purgation, so be it. I needed the nudge. If my serving time inspires others

Protests and Jails

and serves as prophetic witness even through the fog of my own reluctance, I beg God to give me the strength to remain steadfast.

Any time now, my son and daughter-in-law will experience the miracle of childbirth while I wait for further enlightenment, entombed in this dark void. Soon, very soon, my grandchild will emerge into the light of day, breathe a first breath, cry a first prophetic wail announcing *I am arrived!* My arms will ache to cradle that new little life, though I will not be able to do so for many more weeks.

Meanwhile, I'm here on my bunk and the rain is still falling as I peek outside my cell window, glimpsing at the silky patch of grass within my view. Each tender blade quivers with thirsty hope, laboring to become more deeply green. These days too shall pass. In a few months, God will deposit me, a more willing prophet, onto solid ground.

Then the Lord spoke to the great fish and it spewed Jonah out upon the dry land.

—Book of Jonah, 2:10

Afterword

I met Toni Flynn years ago on paper. I unfolded her with care. There she was before me on a page, eight and a half inches by eleven inches. Just the right size for my file folders, but I have never been able to file Toni away. Her essay, found in this book, *Come, Follow Me, A Catholic Worker Introduction*, is the best short piece ever written on Dorothy Day and the Catholic Worker Movement, I venture to say. We at the Open Door Community here in Atlanta, Georgia, use it again and again.

I met Toni Flynn on a rock. We were some 3,000 miles from Atlanta, making a retreat with the Los Angeles Catholic Workers and their sister communities. These folks, including Toni, are among the most radical, steadfast, and prophetic people of faith in the whole wide universe. I was standing on top of a boulder proclaiming the Good News at the top of my lungs: "Y'all are invited to embrace the peace of Jesus!" I could not see anyone nearby, but the California Live Oak trees kept waving their limbs and leaves at me, urging me on. Suddenly, Toni came running up, admonishing me to stop hollering.

Apparently, some people on silent retreat, believing me to be the groundskeeper, had reported to the retreat director, "The gardener has gone mad!" The director guessed (rightly so!) the 'lunatic' might be one of the Catholic Workers, and contacted Toni to intervene. Toni approached me, and gently but firmly reached up and grasped my arm to assist me down from nature's pulpit. "Be quiet, Ed," she insisted. "There are folks here making a silent

Afterword

retreat. The staff is wondering if you have gone crazy". That was the day that she and others at the retreat came to know the John the Baptist side of me! With locust leftovers hanging from my jaw, Toni took me to the chapel to pray quietly for peace and justice.

I met Toni Flynn at the SOAWatch protest in Columbus, Georgia. Toni is spiritually formed and has put on the mantel of God's grace to struggle for peace, truth, righteousness, and she has a readiness to proclaim and practice the non-violent Gospel. Toni Flynn, who would become a grandmother for the first time while behind the gray bars of a cotton-country county jail, stepped over the line at the School of the Americas. Teaching torture and ways to kill the poor and friends of the poor, the School of the Americas is everything the Gospel tells us to leave way behind, or to transform, or to close down. The children of the dead and tortured cry by day and mourn by night for there is no salvation in the land.

Yes, Lord, Toni says to her God, with word and deed. Like Harriet Tubman before her, she takes Exodus steps against Pharaoh telling those in power to let God's people go. She knows she is risking arrest by trespassing onto the Fort Benning military base in the name of peace and justice but she—along with many others—goes forth anyway. She and her fellow non-violent protestors stole the attention of those who were studying how to kill poor villagers, priests, nuns, teachers and labor organizers on that lazy southern sun-filled afternoon.

I met Toni Flynn in jail. Of course, it comes as no surprise to her supporters that she landed in jail on a six-month sentence for trespassing at Fort Benning in the name of peace and justice. It was on Christmas Day when Mike Casey and I filled the Open Door Community box with a crucifix and candle, a loaf of delicious home made bread, a bottle of grape juice, and a Bible. We went off to the Crisp County Jail to offer a liturgy while our community in Atlanta prepared to serve Christmas dinner to 150 homeless and hungry friends. When Mike and I arrived, we were let into the jail and ushered toward the back of a sparse, dimly lit library.

There sat Toni in an orange jumpsuit with her friend and fellow prisoner of conscience, Jerry Zawada, also in orange. They had

Afterword

been confined and outfitted in orange for over five months. After Toni and Jerry shared about jail life, we listened to Luke tell us the Christmas story. Then into the cage came Jesus, broken in bread, poured out in grape juice. We simply sat in silence while gratitude and joy filled the room.

I met Toni Flynn in this book. Her pages in this prophetic reflection, given to us in tested love and faithful action, are fruits of the Spirit. I hope we have listened attentively to this woman's voice and to those for whom she has given a voice, allowing her witness and words to shape to us into radical Disciples of Christ's peace. Toni Flynn, mother and grandmother, who dared to accompany the poor among us, to walk peacefully across lines that kill in order to bring the abundant life for all God's children, has a message for us all—the American Empire and the Mainline Churches notwithstanding.

Eduard Loring

Eduard Loring has authored two books, I Hear Hope Banging At My Back Door *and* The Cry of the Poor. *He is co-founder, with his wife, Murphy Davis, of the Open Door Community in Atlanta Georgia. where they minister to homeless people and those on Death Row. edloriing@opendoorcommunity.org*

We Are Each Other's Angels

I hope I see you later—'cause it's time for me to go
That's my ride that just pulled over—and it sure was good to know you
So go answer your calling—go and fill somebody's cup
And if you see an angel falling—won't you stop and help them up?

   We are each other's angels—we meet when it is time
   We keep each other going—and we show each other signs

Sometimes you'll stumble—sometimes you'll just lie down
Sometimes you'll get lonely—with all these people around
You might shiver when the wind blows—and you might get blown away
You might lose a little color—you might lose a little faith

   We are each other's angels—we meet when it is time
   We keep each other going—and we show each other signs

Thank you for the water—thought I was gonna die out here in the desert but you quenched my thirst
Let's break a little bread together—I've got a little Manna—it was a gift
From someone who was passing by and offered me a lift

   We are each other's angels—we meet when it is time
   We keep each other going—and we show each other signs

Song lyrics by Chuck Brodsky
Used with permission chuck@chuckbrodsky.com

www.ingramcontent.com/pod-product-compliance
Lightning Source LLC
Chambersburg PA
CBHW072142160426
43197CB00012B/2213